BARNES AND MORTLAKE PAST

First published 1997
by Historical Publications Ltd
32 Ellington Street, London N7 8PL
(Tel: 0171-607 1628)

© **Barnes and Mortlake History Society 1997**

ISBN 0 948667 46 X
British Library Cataloguing-in-Publication Data
A catalogue record for this book is available from the British Library

Typeset in Palatino by Historical Publications Ltd
Reproduction by G & J Graphics, EC2
Printed in Zaragoza, Spain by Edelvives

Historical Publications Ltd specialises in local history publishing.
A full list of our publications may be obtained from our
distributors, Phillimore & Co, Shopwyke Manor Barn,
Chichester, Sussex, PO20 6BG.

The publishers would be happy to receive proposals for other
titles in this series.

BARNES AND MORTLAKE PAST

with East Sheen

edited by

Maisie Brown

P.O. TELEPHONE Nº 375 PUTNEY.

S. HOGGER,

STEAM

MOTORS REPAIRED
PAINTED & STORED

ESTABLISHED
1800.

Carriage, Wheel & Motor Works,

12=30 UPPER RICHMOND ROAD,

B.A.R.N.E.S, S.W.

WHEELS TYRED &
RUBBERED ON
THE PREMISES.

MOTOR SPIRIT & LUBRICATING OILS KEPT IN STOCK.

REPAIRS OF EVERY DESCRIPTION

IDEAL TYRES
IF DESIRED.

HISTORICAL PUBLICATIONS

Introduction

Barnes and Mortlake sit side by side on the south bank of the river Thames. Once they were small rural villages in the County of Surrey. Today, they are a part of suburban London, lying to the west of the city, about six miles distant from Hyde Park Corner. The area is essentially residential in character, with a high proportion of good quality, low-density housing, mostly owner-occupied. There is a generous acreage of common and open space within its borders, and a large part of Mortlake parish is in Richmond Park. It is a pleasant place to live, and well placed for daily commuting to inner London.

Barnes occupies around 902 acres. It is bounded on the west by Mortlake, and to the east and south by Putney; the land boundaries, unchanged for centuries, are White Hart Lane, Putney Lower Common and the north side of the Upper Richmond Road, running west from Dyers Lane to Priests Bridge. The northern boundary is the Thames.

The ancient parish of Mortlake with East Sheen once covered some 1,837 acres including 732 acres enclosed in Richmond Park. The old parish boundary ran up the centre of White Hart Lane, along Beverley Brook – a natural boundary with Roehampton – and into Richmond Park. Turning westward it crossed the Lower Pen Pond, then north from the Sidmouth Plantation to Pesthouse Common, along Manor Road, the east side of Sandycombe Lane and back to the river along what is now the west side of the railway embankment to Kew railway bridge. In 1894 the western boundary changed when 329 acres of what is now North Sheen and Kew were transferred to Richmond.

East Sheen is a place of indeterminate boundaries, wholly contained within the parish of Mortlake. Generally speaking, it is the area south of the Upper Richmond Road, but there are many 'grey' areas and any attempt to define where Mortlake ends and East Sheen begins can lead to heated argument. The modern practice of the local council using the railway as the boundary is an administrative convenience and has no historical basis.

Artefacts dating from the prehistoric period are recovered in the area from time to time, but given the present state of knowledge it is impossible to know with any certainty who the first inhabitants were, when they came and how long they stayed. There is, however, little doubt that the manor of Barnes and the manor of Mortlake existed by the late Saxon period. They appear in Domesday Book (1086), listed under their Saxon names, *Berne*, meaning a barn or grange and *Mortelage*, the exact meaning of

which has yet to be decided. One of a number of suggestions is that *lage* (or *lacu*) refers to a watercourse, possibly the Beverley Brook, controlled at its mouth by Morta, a Saxon leader believed to have been in the area. What *is* certain is that Mortlake does not mean the place where Londoners who died in the plague of 1665 were buried, a myth said to have been started by a guide on a passing pleasure boat which has, unfortunately, been widely believed.

There have been times in their history when Barnes and Mortlake have not quite seen eye to eye and to this day each place has its own distinctive and separate character. One thing they do have in common is a site on the Lower Thames within easy reach of London, which on the whole has proved to be an advantage. From earliest time, the river was of vital importance to both places for transport, communication and fishing. The presence of a major route to and from London, literally on the doorstep, gave early opportunities for trading with the capital; and as London grew the opportunities increased. In the seventeenth century market gardening began in Barnes and Mortlake in response to the growing demands of the London market. At the same time the first of a number of small industries appeared on the riverside at Mortlake, sited as close as possible to the Thames – a natural highway for raw materials and finished goods.

The river brought visitors from London. Illustrious people were known to arrive at the river landing places in Barnes and Mortlake long before the seventeenth century. By the eighteenth century London was regarded as an increasingly unhealthy place, and more of its wealthier citizens chose to settle in the area, giving a welcome boost to the local economy.

The influence of London can be seen to have played a part in the economic and social development of both Barnes and Mortlake in previous centuries, but it was not until the latter half of the nineteenth century that the two villages came to be totally dominated by the metropolis. Until the early part of that century the lack of a direct road link to London had ensured that the area remained something of a rural backwater, especially with regard to Barnes. But two major events – the opening of the first Hammersmith Bridge in 1827 and the coming of the railway in 1846 – caused the inevitable changes which led to the transformation from small villages to pleasant suburbs of London. When a Charter of Incorporation was granted in 1932, the entire area became the Borough of Barnes, which in April 1965 was absorbed into the London Borough of Richmond upon Thames.

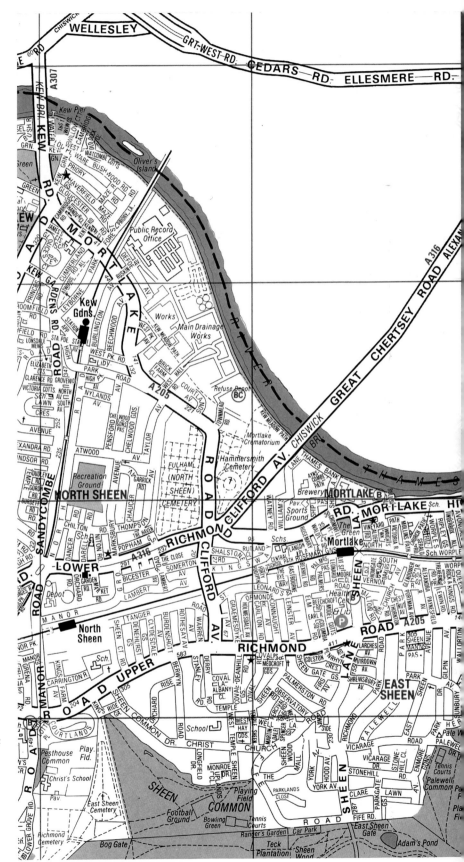

This modern map of the Barnes, Mortlake and East Sheen area is reproduced by kind permission of the London Borough of Richmond upon Thames.

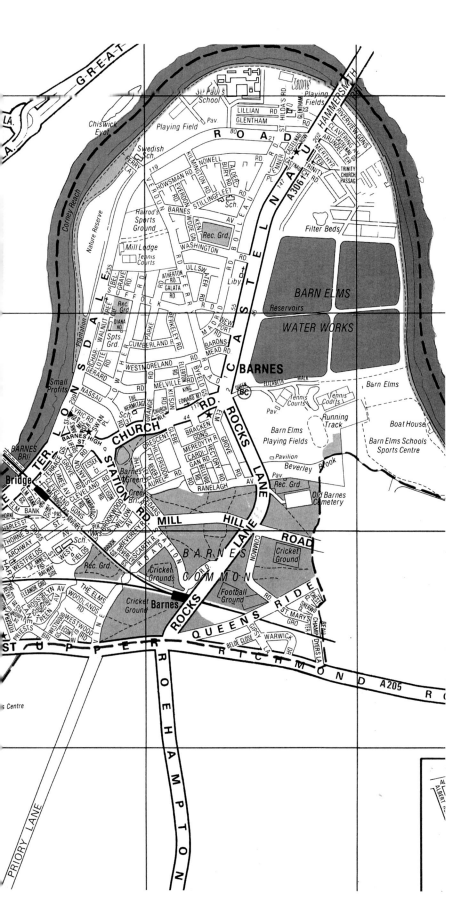

1. *A south view of Barnes c.1750, showing the windmill on the Common at Mill Hill and Barnes church. To the left of the church can be seen the Rectory (now Strawberry House) and to the right the Homestead, both of which still stand. To the right of the Homestead is Byfield House and in front can be seen the conduit. Engraving by J. Roberts after J.B. Chatelain.*

Beginnings

EARLY PEOPLE

Evidence of prehistoric occupation is particularly strong in the Mortlake area, where numerous artefacts have been found in that part of the Thames reach. These have included several flint axes and a 'pick' of the Mesolithic period (*c*.8,000-4,500 BC), and a complete pottery bowl of the Neolithic period (*c*.4,500-3,500 BC), found near the Ship Inn at Thames Bank. In 1977 a rare Palaeolithic (Stone Age) hand axe was recovered near Mortlake Brewery, also a

occupation in Barnes were found when trenches were dug for a new gas terminal beneath the Barn Elms playing fields, leading to the discovery of what could be an important Middle Iron Age settlement of the lowland hillfort type. Quernstones and other signs of habitation, such as waste pits and postholes, were found. A bi-conical ceramic bead, possibly a spindle whorl used in spinning wool, came from the workmen's waste tip.

ROMANS AND SAXONS

It is possible that part of the Upper Richmond Road is Roman in origin. From Priests Bridge to Sheen Lane, the roadway passed between two cultivated strips of land in the Mortlake commonfield, Strat Furlong Shot and Above Strat Furlong (*strat* or *straet* is a Saxon word meaning a 'Roman' or ancient highway).

Though Roman remains have been found in nearby Putney, until recently only a few had been found in either Barnes or Mortlake, These were a burial urn containing cremated human bone fragments, either Late Iron Age or of the Romano/British period, found immediately below the modern surface on Mill Hill, Barnes Common in 1950, plus a few abraded sherds of what might be Roman pottery, recovered during demolition work at Mortlake Green School in 1990. But current archaeological work on 25km of Thames shore between Teddington Lock and the Beverley Brook has uncovered fish-traps at Barn Elms which may prove to date from the late Romano/British period.

The small number of Saxon sites found in Surrey is said to result from wholesale destruction in the nineteenth century when their importance was not

2. Neolithic (c.4500-3500 BC) pottery bowl found in the river at Mortlake.

Late Bronze Age sword from around the seventh century BC and an iron dagger in a bronze-bound sheath, dating from the sixth century BC. A Late Bronze Age socketed spear head was found just upstream of Barnes Railway Bridge in 1992.

Items taken from the river are not necessarily related to a nearby settlement and land finds are obviously more meaningful. For example, flint tools from the Mesolithic period found on Barnes Common near Mill Hill in December 1977, are seen as evidence of a nearby settlement. Further signs of prehistoric

3. Iron dagger in bronze-bound sheath found in the Thames at Mortlake. (Late Bronze Age.)

and was joined by another running from the High Street towards the river. Both contained pottery sherds which, subject to further dating, are thought to be from the Roman period.

After the Saxon period however, there are few signs of occupation until the sixteenth century, except some building refuse and pottery of the late thirteenth-fifteenth century. Dating from the mid-sixteenth century were the remains of a timber-framed building fronting the High Street, with a gravel surfaced yard or path sloping towards the river. Other finds on the site were the remains of a river revetment, later industrial buildings and the eighteenth-century malthouse which may be seen in Leigh's Panorama of the Thames, published in 1820. There may be more to find on this rewarding site, and to the west other demolition sites will shortly be available for investigation, so that evidence of continuous settlement in one area of Mortlake may yet emerge.

THE SITE

Barnes and Mortlake are sited on the northern edge of the Kempton Park floodplain terrace. The glacial Thames sand and gravel terraces are believed to have been laid down no later than the last Ice Age (*c*.10,000 BC). The natural soil in the floodplain area, a mixture of sand, gravel and London clay, is light and reasonably fertile.

Mortlake lies at the bottom of a southern meander of the Thames. The land rises gently southward from the river towards the higher ground in East Sheen and the hills of Richmond Park. The Mortlake high point, 165 feet, is near the northern tip of Sidmouth Wood within the Park.

In Barnes the terrain is almost uniformly flat; the high point is at Mill Hill on Barnes Common, a mere 27ft above flood level. The greater part of Barnes, including Barn Elms, the former manorial estate, is a peninsula, bordered on three sides by a pronounced bend in the Thames. Much of its southern base is traversed by the furthermost reach of the Beverley Brook. The peninsula is mainly alluvium, but a wide area of gravel and sand on its western side gives firm landing at low tide. The gravel persists along Barnes Terrace and the riverside at Mortlake, giving way to alluvium beyond Thames Bank. The wide gravelly foreshore would have been an ideal landing place for early settlers, more especially since for much of the prehistoric period and beyond, the Thames was non-tidal above Westminster, with a normal level much the same as today's low tide.

generally realised. This might explain why so little Saxon material has been found in Barnes and Mortlake. An eighth-century iron bell and several iron spearheads, found on the foreshore at Mortlake in 1992, are among the few artefacts recovered. However, in May 1996, the remains of two Saxon sunken-featured buildings were found on a demolition site by the riverside in Mortlake High Street, one with an associated and virtually complete fired clay oven, possibly a bread oven. This is the first tangible evidence of a Saxon settlement in Mortlake.

On the same site the first sign of prehistoric occupation in Mortlake was also found. This consisted of circular and rectilinear pits containing pottery sherds dating from the Late Bronze/Early Iron Age. It is possible that the pits relate to a settlement covering the entire site. Also found were two ditches dug through gravel and silt: one ran parallel to the river

The Manors

The manors of Mortlake and Barnes were established some time before the Norman Conquest of 1066. Barnes, formerly part of the manor of Mortlake, was a separate manor by AD 939. Both manors were in the Brixton Hundred, a north-eastern division of Surrey which was, on the basis of population density, the most prosperous part of the county. It contained the largest area of cultivated land, some highly valued manors and the important borough of Southwark.

THE MANOR OF MORTLAKE

The Domesday Book of 1086 was concerned with the worth of manors and estates, rather than with villages. Of the eighteen manors in Brixton Hundred, the manor of Mortlake was third highest in value and fifth highest in the entire county of Surrey. It was held by the Archbishop of Canterbury, and its assets included two mills, seventeen houses in London and four in Southwark; there was also a church and a fishery. As well as Mortlake itself, the manor included the area later known as East Sheen, the vill of Putney and the hamlets of Wimbledon and Roehampton.

Domesday records the vast manor of Mortlake having land sufficient for the yearly use of 35 ploughs, with 33 in use in 1086. Five ploughlands were in demesne (land reserved for the lord's own use), scattered throughout the manor, and 28 were given over to the tenants. Typically, a ploughland was around 120 acres of arable land, giving a total of 3960 acres under cultivation. In contrast to this, meadowland – essential for providing winter animal feed – amounted to just twenty acres, pointing to an economy based on arable farming, rather than animal husbandry. Waste or common land is not mentioned. The actual measure of woodland is not given, but the number of swine due to the Archbishop – 55, probably one in ten of the number present – suggests that there was sufficient woodland to support 550 pigs.

As to population, Domesday lists eighty villeins, fourteen bordars and sixteen serfs. It is here recording the number of people obliged to provide work services to the Archbishop, so if a typical family numbered four or five people, then the total population was around 500. Spread over the entire manor

4. *The medieval tithe barn which stood on the river side of Mortlake High Street. It was demolished c.1865 and the site incorporated into the brewery.*

5. Text of the Domesday entry for Mortlake and Barnes, 1086.

the figure does not appear to be high, but compared with the low Surrey average, the manor was well populated. Despite that, the amount of land given over to crops indicates a surplus of produce above subsistence level and it seems highly probable that the manor was selling surplus grain to London.

As the manor was named Mortlake, it is reasonable to suppose that Mortlake itself was the largest village. It contained the manor house and, very probably, the Domesday church, since in the early medieval period the parish church was almost always built close to the manor house. Mortlake's manor house stood on four acres of land east of Ship Lane, a site now occupied by the old brewery buildings. From the eleventh to the early fifteenth century a succession of Archbishops of Canterbury stayed at the house – nine died there. And judging by the number of monarchs who visited their Archbishops, including Kings John, Edward II and Edward III, the manor house was a place of some importance. In the fourteenth century, however, Mortlake was overtaken by Wimbledon and the manor became known as the manor of Wimbledon.

The accession of Henry VIII brought Mortlake's long association with the Archbishops to an end. In 1536 Henry took the manor into his own hands, giving it first to Thomas Cromwell, who enlarged the manor house, and after Cromwell's execution, to

Catherine Parr. Henry is remembered in Mortlake as the king who ordered the removal of the parish church from its site near the manor house to its present position in the High Street in 1543.

The manor stayed in royal hands until 1576, when it was granted to Sir Thomas Cecil. Cecil chose to build a far grander manor house at Wimbledon and the old house at Mortlake gradually fell into decay – there is some evidence that during the seventeenth century the gatehouse was in use as an inn. By the eighteenth century only ruins remained to be demolished.

The last lords of the manor of Wimbledon *alias* Mortlake in the true sense were the Spencers, who acquired it in 1744. The title, which carries no legal rights, was put up for auction by the present Earl Spencer in July 1996 and was sold to an anonymous buyer.

EAST SHEEN AND WESTHALL

There is no mention of East Sheen in Domesday, but by the thirteenth century it is noted in records as a subordinate manor within the manor of Mortlake. To the west of the village of Mortlake was an estate called Westhall, which was linked with East Sheen, so that the small sub-manor was always known as the manor of East Sheen and Westhall. About 1500, the estate became freehold when the lords of the manor, the Welbecks, secured their independence from Mortlake. In modern terms, the early manor house was situated on the west side of Sheen Lane near the junction with Christchurch Road, but by the end of the eighteenth century it was superseded by West Park, a house in Westhall.

THE MANOR OF BARNES

Barnes was a single village manor, granted to the Dean and Chapter of St Paul's Cathedral by the Saxon King Athelstan (*r*. 924-939). In 1086, there was enough land for six ploughs of which five were in use – two in demesne and three let to tenants. Nine villeins and four bordars are noted, giving a population of around sixty.

For a small manor Barnes had a large amount of meadowland, listed as twenty acres, but in fact just over twelve of these are believed to have belonged to the manor of Mortlake, dating from the time when Barnes was part of the larger manor. Meadowland by the riverside at Barnes, known as Westmead or Lottmead, was divided into more or less equal lots and shared among the Putney tenants; in time it became known as 'Putney Detached', and it was not until 1906 that it was officially declared to be part of Barnes. Part of the land is now occupied by the Leg of Mutton Wildfowl Reserve.

6. *Barn Elms, the former manor house of Barnes. The block built by Thomas Cartwright in 1694 is in the centre; wings were added in 1770 and there were many later additions. After the Second World War the house became derelict and was demolished in 1954 after being damaged by fire.*

The revenue and produce from the demesne land was used to support and sustain those living within the cathedral, via two of the St Paul's canons. Three times a year deliveries of grain to make bread and beer were taken to the cathedral, together with any surplus produce. The canons were, in effect, the lords of the manor, but in practice were absentee landlords, residing at St Paul's. It is doubtful if they ever so much as set foot on their Barnes land, which was always sub-let to a manager or farmer who, to all intents and purposes, ran the manor.

This system continued until some time in the fifteenth century, most probably 1467, when St Paul's leased the estate to Sir John Saye, Chancellor of the Exchequer to Edward IV, the first of a long line of lay tenants. But apart from the Commonwealth period, when Church lands were sequestered to Parliament, the freehold of the estate and certain areas of Barnes remained in the hands of the cathedral chapter for several centuries. The last few freeholds of property built on Church land were sold shortly after World War II.

BARN ELMS

Barn Elms, the manor house, stood on the east side of the Barnes peninsula near the river on the demesne estate, which extended to the Common on the south and the road to Chiswick ferry on the north-west, an area of about 463 acres. Queen Elizabeth I visited the house to see her Secretary of State, Sir Francis Walsingham, who held the lease from 1579 until his death in 1590. Sometimes the Queen's visits were private, at others she came with her court. During this colourful period in its history, Barn Elms was the scene of affairs of state: Councils were held and policies formed. 'Spy-master' Walsingham's secretary, Robert Beale, lived conveniently close by at Milbourne House and it is not difficult to imagine the plotting and intriguing which went on at the manor house. Beale it was who carried the order for the execution of Mary, Queen of Scots, to Fotheringay and witnessed the Queen's beheading.

A survey of the house taken on behalf of Cromwell in 1641 records the mansion by then split into five dwellings. There were two farms on the estate, Home Farm on the east of the peninsula near the house, and Windmill Farm to the west, the site of the present day Harrodian School. The remainder of the estate was split into small closes leased to five farmers, of whom at least two were market gardeners. Exactly when the medieval house was built and what it looked like is not known, other than that it was of brick and timber, but it must have been impressive as in 1664 it was taxed on possessing 23 hearths.

In 1694 the lessee, Thomas Cartwright of Aynho, Northants, demolished the old house and replaced it with a smaller structure, which he sub-let and which stood for 260 years.

7. *Barnes parish church from the north-east. An unusual view of the church which, except for the blocking of the east windows and the addition of the tower c.1485, is unchanged from 1215. Drawing by Samuel Hieronymus Grimm, 1773.*

The Three Villages

ORIGINS

Barnes began as a 'green' village, that is, it was centred on a green near the point where the present Church Road, Station Road and the High Street meet. The Great Pond, known today as Barnes Pond, was one of three on the Green, and anciently owned by St Paul's Cathedral, but in 1388 the pond together with another, was granted to the newly-designated Barnes Rector.

The High Street, called Barnes Street by 1700, was the way from the Green to the river docking place mentioned in 1400 as *le new docke*. The present bend in the High Street may well have been shaped by medieval farmers as year after year they guided their oxen and ploughs around some immovable obstruction, possibly a tree root, because the pathway to the river was also the path between the two great open fields of Barnes.

Mortlake, on the other hand, was a 'street' village, with dwellings on one side of the highway. The Saxon settlement is believed to have been near the landing place (*le wharfe*) on Thames Bank, west of Ship Lane, with smaller communities to the east. When the manor house and church were built they were sited east of Ship Lane and from the later pattern of development it seems that the village grew up alongside the manor house and church, then extended slowly eastward in a ribbon development along the High Street. Between the High Street and the river, a back lane (Thames Street) ran from the Lower Richmond Road to the towing path and another landing place, the town wharf.

Documentary evidence of medieval East Sheen is sparse. In 1247 it was a hamlet of Mortlake, and early areas of settlement appear to have been around Milestone Green at the foot of the hill where Sheen Lane meets the Upper Richmond Road – a spot long regarded as the centre of East Sheen – and around the Plough in Christchurch Road. The name East Sheen, meaning east of Sheen, may be traced back to the time when Richmond was called Shene – Henry VII renamed it after his Earldom of Richmond in Yorkshire. East Sheen itself was not affected by this as it was part of the Archbishop of Canterbury's land.

8. *A Fair in Mortlake High Street, c.1772. (From a painting by S.H. Grimm.)*

COMMON FIELDS

Between the eleventh and thirteenth centuries the system of farming large open fields was adopted in Barnes and Mortlake. Under the control of the manor court, tenants were permitted to farm strips in the fields in return for obligatory services on the manorial demesne land. Tenant holdings consisted of a number of strips scattered throughout the fields, to ensure that everybody had a share of both poor and fertile lands. Details of individual holdings were recorded in the court rolls, with the tenant having a copy – thus his tenancy was called copyhold.

Barnes, it seems, had a basic two-field arrangement: the Westfield, which lay to the south of the High Street, and the Northfield on the opposite side. The latter stretched back towards the road to Chiswick Ferry, served by two worple ways, Norton Lane (now Grange Road) and Bagley's Stile, which survives in part on the pavements of the Lowther Estate. Westfield

went from today's Terrace to Vine Road and between White Hart Lane, High Street and Station Road. A trackway, which survives as Thorne Passage, ran diagonally across, providing a convenient and dry route from Mortlake to Barnes if the river was in flood.

According to an Inquisition of 1222 the largest tenant holding in Barnes was a virgate, roughly fifteen acres, and the smallest two to ten acres, whose tenants were not all wholly dependent upon the land, since they included a carter, blacksmith, two fishermen and a shepherd who attended the demesne flock.

Mortlake's main fields were Northfield, from the High Street to Pale Lane (partly Park Avenue now), and Southfield, now mostly in Stonehill, the upper part of East Sheen and Richmond Park. Two smaller fields were Clay Ends and Fortie.

In both parishes the change from communal farm-

9. *Mortlake, c.1825. The viewpoint is from Thames Bank looking east with Castelnau House on the extreme left (the bend of the river has been exaggerated). Lithograph by Charles King of Mortlake.*

ing to enclosed holdings was a gradual process, beginning in the sixteenth century. There is no doubt that the development of market gardens hastened it to such an extent that a Parliamentary Enclosure Act – common in many parishes around London – was not needed in the eighteenth century. Milne's *Land Use Map of London and its Environs*, published in 1800, shows large areas of enclosed market garden land in Barnes and Mortlake, and apart from vestiges of a strip pattern to the south of Mortlake High Street, nothing remained of the common fields.

THE VILLAGES DEVELOP

At the beginning of the seventeenth century there were probably around 150 to 200 people living in Barnes and 400 in Mortlake with East Sheen. A survey of the manor of Wimbledon (1617) records 79 houses in Mortlake parish, of which 26 were in East Sheen, including its manor house. East Sheen also included the homes of four of the largest land-owners in the parish. The small hamlet by then had advanced from Milestone Green, past the Dogge inn and along Sheen Lane to today's Christchurch Road and Temple Sheen.

In Mortlake village, four large houses were on Thames Bank, including Leyden House, dating from Tudor times and happily still standing, together with an inn. Five houses stood on the grounds of the old manor house. Dwellings on the north side of the High Street extended as far east as the boundary with Barnes, a mixture of small cottages and large houses. On the south side, the church and thirteen dwellings had been built on Ewe furlong, the common field area

10. West Hall. A late seventeenth-century house which stands in West Hall Road, off Mortlake Road. It was one of the principal houses of the manor of East Sheen and Westhall. Much of this area of the parish was transferred to Richmond in 1894.

nearest to the Thames, bounded by the High Street, White Hart Lane, Sheen Lane and the Worple Way. (Ewe comes from the Saxon *ea*, meaning water.)

In Barnes, Milbourne House stood facing the pond. A house of that name has stood on the site since the fifteenth century; old Essex House was nearby. There were at least two inns in the village by 1637 – the Beare and the Rose near the pond end of the High Street. Possibly a house known as the Mansion House was to its right; its west wing survives as a small shop, no. 1 Church Road. A straggle of cottages was on the south side of the High Street, and others were making their way along the road to the church.

VILLAGE TRAUMAS

Two important events occurred in Mortlake in the first half of the seventeenth century which had far-reaching effects. First was the decision of James I to establish a tapestry works there, in which fifty Flemish weavers (the first contingent of a total of 140) were employed, many with wives and children.

Then, in 1637, Mortlake saw 732 acres of its land disappear behind the newly completed wall of Charles I's new hunting park. In all, six parishes lost land to Richmond Park, but in terms of acreage Mortlake's loss was the greatest. Generally the land lost was common land and private closes, and though the King paid generously for his appropriation it was unpopular, and no doubt some quiet cheers were raised for Parliament when the Civil War began.

No Civil War battles were fought in Barnes and Mortlake, but the taxes imposed by Parliament to pay for the army were the highest ever known. Parish account books show that for a while the two villages were adept at avoiding payment of the Weekly Assessment, a tax levied on each person apart from the very poor. Later, however, taxes were collected with greater efficiency. There was also excise to be paid on many commodities, the obligation to supply provisions to troops, and in 1642-5 soldiers and their horses were billeted on the villagers of Mortlake and Barnes.

Early on in the war Barnes lost its Rector, a high church Cambridge graduate, called John Cutts, who beat a hasty retreat to Oxford to join the King. But records of the Hearth Tax imposed in 1664, after the monarchy was restored, show that Barnes and Mortlake had made gains, despite the war, in population and in middle class homes.

In Barnes 84 households were liable for the tax and nine unable to pay, which suggests a population of around 400. Just over 4% of the households were in the upper gentry class, with more than ten hearths; below them the yeoman and lower gentry class made up around 30%, then came husbandmen, small farmers, craftsmen and tradesmen at 40%, leaving about 24% in the labouring class.

11. Barnes Terrace, 1823. The view is from the White Hart with Waring's Brewery and the wall of St Ann's in the distance. Lithograph by W. Westall.

12. *Barnes Terrace, 14 August 1827. Looking west with Waring's brewery on the left, the end of the High Street and No. 3 The Terrace to the right of the mast of the barge. From a pencil drawing by E.W. Cooke.*

13. *The west end of Lonsdale Road and the Terrace, Barnes, in 1896. To the left is the tower of St Ann's, next the Bull's Head and Waterman's Arms, and the end of the High Street. The houses in the Terrace are still recognisable. Note the complete absence of a river wall. Wash drawing by S. Kay in the Paton Collection*

Malt House

Mortlake Church

14. *Mortlake river front c.1820. The house to the right of the church tower still stands, next to it is the Lower Dutch House of the Tapestry Works, separated by an alley from the Queen's Head. From Samuel Leigh's Panorama of the Thames.*

In Mortlake and East Sheen, the number of houses had risen from 79 in 1617 to 205, suggesting a population of over 900; the same upward trend is revealed in neighbouring parishes such as Wimbledon and Putney. The larger houses, as in 1617, were still in East Sheen, but one, an inn owned by Cecily Berry was in Mortlake: her probate inventory of 1670 lists five rooms on the ground floor and seven chambers above. Of the rest, 48 houses contained 4-9 hearths, 105 2-3, and 36 had only one or none at all.

A final trauma that century was the Great Plague of 1665. The Mortlake burial register records 207 deaths against a yearly average of 29 over the previous decade, the first death noted being that of the wife of a waterman, whose husband may well have brought the disease from London. Fourteen members of the English family died in Mortlake between August and October. In Barnes the burial register has small black crosses against eighteen names.

15. *Acacia House, a fine 18th-century house which still stands beside the river in the High Street.*

Head   Mor...

NEW INFLUENCES

In the seventeenth century the most marked change in the area was the growth of market gardens and orchards in place of arable farming. Men like Robert Burges and Richard Edwards of Barnes did well from their market gardens, living in large well-furnished farmhouses. Edwards had land in Barnes, Roehampton and Teddington and in one two-acre field he grew asparagus worth £50 an acre.

Local prosperity was accompanied by an increase in the number of small traders, craftsmen, shops and inns. Barnes had a blacksmith, baker, wheelwright, a shop selling 'lumber', and a nurseryman, William

Blinde, who catered for a wealthy clientele. In Blinde's probate inventory, all "the ordinary sorts of flowers" are lumped together, but the highly prized "florists flowers" such as auriculas, ranunculus, tulips and anemones are carefully listed. These then were expensive rarities. Mortlake had its own garden centre. Samuel Hussey, nurseryman and plantsman must have been one of the wealthiest traders in the parish. A specialist in evergreen shrubs and rare trees, he too had large stocks of "florists flowers". His six-roomed house was furnished with the modest luxury items of the day, such as three feather beds, mirrors, books, a long case clock and silver spoons, and he owned a watch worth eighteen guineas. Like Blinde, the size and nature of his business indicates that customers came from a wide area.

Mortlake also had two carpenters, a glazier, blacksmith, paver, a house painter and two shoemakers.

Not every year was prosperous. Watermen were particularly badly hit in the 1690s when the Thames froze for weeks on end in several winters. In Barnes the yearly cost of poor relief rose steadily from £24 in 1690 to £96 in 1695. In the latter year, the Rector, William Richardson, explained that "Our poor rate hath risen upon us for some late years by reason that several children have to the relief of the Parish, their fathers, being watermen, dying very poor."

When the first census was taken in 1801, Barnes had a population of 860 and 170 houses. Mortlake with East Sheen had 1,748 people and 301 houses. This was not a vast increase on the seventeenth century and life had changed little. But there had been a gradual reversal in the respective roles of the manor courts and the parish vestry. Apart from the registration of land transactions, the manor courts lost their control over day-to-day life. The parishes on the other hand were given more and more responsibilities, from the care of the poor to the maintenance of highways, and this trend was to continue throughout the nineteenth century.

When the 1838 Tithe Maps of the villages were drawn up, there was still a vast amount of open space, the buildings confined mostly to a series of small ribbon developments, except the large houses south of the Upper Richmond Road which stood in their own ample grounds.

On the map of Barnes there is, however, a sign of things to come. The only buildings on the peninsula are Barn Elms, Barn Elms Farm and Mill Farm, but a new wide road runs up its centre towards Hammersmith Bridge.

16. *Mortlake, May 1821. Viewed from Thames Bank looking east, with Ashleigh House in the distance, the parish church in the centre and the gazebo of Cromwell House. To the right is Riverside House, the home of the artist, Ann Maria Best.*

17. *Mud Cottages prior to demolition in 1903. These early nineteenth-century cottages stood on the corner of St Leonard's Road opposite William's Cottages and their dereliction contrasts with the well-groomed Joseph Newman, caretaker of The Limes (then the Council House).*

Fertile Fields

Towards the end of the reign of Elizabeth I, fruit and vegetables, once neglected items, became popular with the wealthier London citizens who demanded such luxuries as green peas, garden beans and carrots. In response, a trickle of garden produce began to arrive in the City from the nearby Thames-side villages, and by the mid-seventeenth century, when the population of London was approaching half a million, the trickle had increased to a stream of some proportion.

At that time the economy of Barnes and Mortlake revolved around the land and its produce, as it had for generations. Though there had been a modest increase in the number of local occupations, agriculture and the transport of its produce was still the main means of earning a living. However, change lay in the produce itself. Profits from fruit and vegetables were high and arable farmers in Barnes, Mortlake and East Sheen were quick to respond to the growing demands of London. Neat rows of vegetables and salad crops, and fruit orchards underplanted with soft-fruit bushes, replaced fields of wheat and barley. Market gardening was destined to feature in the area for some 230 years.

In *The General Views of Agriculture in the Counties of England* (1790), one surveyor, William Stevenson, remarked on the immense quantities of high quality asparagus produced in Barnes and Mortlake, together with a wide variety of other vegetables and fruits destined for Covent Garden market. The *Gentleman's Magazine* for January 1797 records the death of Richard Adams, gardener of East Sheen, who "cultivated 40 acres of asparagus for the London market and was known to receive £300 in one day for this article at Covent Garden."

According to Stevenson, the gardeners used every inch of growing space available for continuous cash-cropping. "To achieve the state of high fertility necessary", he noted, the gardeners had access to an unlimited supply of what they euphemistically termed 'London Muck', made from the droppings of the capital's horses, waste matter from its slaughter houses, sugar bakers and tallow chandlers, and nightsoil from its privies. Stevenson describes in loving detail how this rich, well-rotted manure was carried in waggons from "the grand depository", St George's Fields, Southwark, loaded onto Thames barges and transported to wharves along the river where market gardeners carted it to their grounds to be spread at a rate of 80 tons per acre. Locally, gardeners collected their supplies from the Dung Wharf, sited near the present day council refuse depot at Townmead Road, and from Town Wharf off Mortlake High Street. Manure which found its way into the river brought complaints from villagers whose

18. A farmhouse at East Sheen, 1833. The house, much altered, still stands in Fife Road by the entrance to Sheen Common.

19. John Biggs (1757-1837), market gardener of Barnes and Mortlake, here shown surveying his land in the old open fields of Mortlake, with Mortlake church in the distance. From a painting dated 1833 by E.W. Cooke.

water supply came from the Thames, especially during outbreaks of cholera which occurred from time to time. It was also hinted that the barges which brought the muck from London, were the same barges which carried the produce back to the metropolis.

Men were employed in the gardens on a regular basis, for ploughing, digging, carting and spreading manure, but the seasonal jobs – planting, weeding and gathering, washing and packing – were performed by women casual labourers.

The majority of the workforce was local, but in the soft-fruit season much of the carrying work was done by young girls from Shropshire and Wales. In the winter these girls worked in the coalpits, but the wages in fruit-picking compared well with work at the mines, and these tough young women walked to Covent Garden in droves, with baskets of fruit weighing from forty to fifty pounds on their heads, sometimes making several trips a day. In *A Morning's Walk from London to Kew* (1816), Sir Richard Phillips mentions conversing with Shropshire girls in the local gardens. The *Richmond Herald* noted them still

at work in 1879, but from the mid 1840s, a high proportion of the casual labour was provided by young Irish men and women in flight from the horrors of the potato famine. The Shropshire girls mostly came for the season, but many of the young Irish stayed on to become a permanent part of the local population.

The opening of the first Hammersmith Bridge in 1827 was a sad day for local watermen, for the gardeners then had a direct road route to London and did most of their own carting. John Biggs, a leading market gardener in Barnes and Mortlake, owned ten market carts, several waggons and twelve draught horses when he died in 1837. In that same year, the Tithe Commissioner reported that the wealth of the parishes of Barnes and Mortlake was in their market gardens. Out of 485 acres of arable land in Mortlake, 432 were used for market gardens, and in Barnes the respective figures were 400 and 200. Even then, much of the remaining land was used to provide feed for the gardeners' horses. The "light sandy topsoil had been radically changed, so as to be ren-

20. Market gardens in Blind Lane (now Temple Sheen Road), East Sheen, 1903. Drawing by W. Lewis Turner.

dered perfectly artificial, the resulting twelve inches of rich black topsoil shows not a vestige of its original formation." The change was judged to be due to the "extravagant use" of "manure obtained from London."

There were then twelve market gardeners in Barnes and 23 in Mortlake and East Sheen, with holdings ranging from 152 acres down to two to three. In Barnes, strip farming had long given way to the irregular pattern of market garden enclosures.

William Lobjoit had a ten acre field on the manorial estate near Hammersmith Bridge and another seventeen acres behind the parish workhouse, an enclosure from the common. Several smallholders were alongside the road to the bridge (now Castelnau), and behind them was open farmland.

In Mortlake, garden ground covered most of the land north of the Lower Richmond Road, between the river and what is now Sandycombe Lane, and to the west of Sheen Lane between the Upper and Lower Richmond Roads and Manor Road. Smaller areas were to the south of the Upper Richmond Road in East Sheen.

The zenith of market gardens was in the 1880s. Each night from around 10pm a steady stream of loaded waggons crossed Hammersmith Bridge bound for Covent Garden. Yet by the turn of the century the end was in sight, for the fact was that few of the gardeners owned their own land, and when it became more valuable for building development landowners took advantage of the situation.

A few local gardeners survived into the second decade of the twentieth century. Some lucky householders will still find wild asparagus and rhubarb sprouting in their gardens, while others have fine old fruit trees.

21. A market garden off Bridge Road (now Castelnau) mid 19th century. Female labourers pack strawberries into pottles for market, while others gather fruit from the fields. From the Illustrated London News, 1846.

The Mortlake Tapestry Works

Mortlake's most illustrious industry, the Tapestry Works, was established in 1619 under the patronage of James I. Henry IV of France had started a similar venture in Paris in 1607 and there can be little doubt that its success impressed the Stuart court. There were two factors which made the choice of Mortlake for a tapestry works justifiable: its site by the river ensured a degree of humidity essential in weaving in order to relax the tension on the warp, while the river itself provided a satisfactory means of transporting the bulky products.

The enterprise was a private one, albeit with royal encouragement. It was run by Sir Francis Crane, secretary to the Prince of Wales, and a successful business man. Crane provided the buildings and equipment and engaged the workforce; in return, as initial capital, he was given £2,000 plus the revenues from the sale of three baronetcies, probably amounting to around £2,100 apiece. Flemish weavers, renowned as the finest craftsmen in Europe, were recruited and during 1620, 140 weavers and their families arrived in Mortlake. The well-respected Philip de Maecht was lured from his post as master weaver at the French works, to fill the same position at Mortlake, and work began on the first commission, a set of nine tapestries for the Prince of Wales depicting the Amours of Vulcan and Venus. Each piece, approx. 15 x 20ft, was woven in wool and silk and lavishly embellished with gold and silver thread. The set was begun on 16 September 1620 and completed by 5 June 1622.

In 1623 two events helped to consolidate the venture and establish its international reputation. The first was the acquisition of the 'Acts of the Apostles'

22. Mortlake tapestry: Venus and Vulcan. From the earliest set woven at Mortlake for the Prince of Wales, 1622.

23. Francis Cleyn (1590-1658), limner or principal designer to the Tapestry Works. Engraving by T. Chambars.

24. Sir Francis Crane (c.1579-1636), first director of the Tapestry Works. Engraving after Van Dyck.

cartoons, commissioned by Pope Leo X and drawn by Raphael in 1515, as designs for tapestries for the Sistine Chapel. The surviving seven of the original ten were up for auction in Genoa and were bought by the Prince of Wales' agents, specifically for use at Mortlake. They are now rated as the finest examples of Renaissance art in the Royal Collection. Next came the appointment of Francis Cleyn, as master painter and designer. Cleyn, a native of Rostock, was given a specially built house opposite the main tapestry works, west of the parish church. He lived there for many years with his wife and family, close to a number of smaller cottages built for the weavers. His first task was to make full-scale working drawings of the Raphael cartoons and to re-design the borders. The series was tremendously popular, as were the many other designs by Cleyn, including the Hero and Leander and the Five Senses series. The working partnership of Cleyn and de Maecht, combined with the skill of the weavers and the determination of Crane to set a high standard of excellence, ensured that the tapestries woven during the next twenty years were of a quality and artistry unrivalled in Europe.

The Tapestry Works was made up of several buildings, the most important being "two brick piles" mentioned in a survey taken in 1651. The larger of the two, known as the Lower Dutch House, stood

facing the river immediately opposite the parish church. This marked the western boundary of the works and was a multi-storied structure with basement sub-structure and watergate to the river. On the second floor was the "great working room" equipped with horizontal looms. The remaining three floors contained one and two-roomed apartments for the weavers, possibly intended for young bachelors, several of whom were to marry into local families. The smaller of the two buildings, the Upper Dutch House, marked the eastern boundary of the works. It had a workroom with looms, "a great working room" for Cleyn, and more apartments for the weavers. In a courtyard between the two main houses stood a house for the master weaver and ancillary buildings. There was also a small chapel erected specially for the weavers, who were mostly Dutch Lutherans – a special dispensation from the Archbishop of Canterbury allowed them to worship there in their own way, with the qualification that the service had to be in Dutch.

During its relatively short life, the output of the works was prodigious, yet despite the excellence of its products, which were highly acclaimed, it was rarely a financial success. The royal patrons and their friends placed lavish orders, but once the lengthy business of weaving a set of tapestries was completed, they were slow to pay for them, often running

25. A Mortlake tapestry – 'The Miraculous Draught of Fishes' from the series of the Acts of the Apostles.

up huge debts. Meanwhile, bills for expensive materials and running costs had to be met by Crane. Since the business had been under-capitalised from the start, this meant an almost permanent lack of cash.

Crane was several times on the verge of financial ruin, saved only by last minute injections of royal cash, but it was the weavers who were the true sufferers. Unable to return to the Netherlands for fear of religious persecution by the ruling Spaniards, they stayed on to endure long periods of hardship, often coming close to starvation from lack of pay. At the same time they refused to compromise on their high standards of workmanship.

There was a dramatic improvement in 1636, when Crane died and Charles I bought the business. From then on it was the King's Works and there followed a short period of unprecedented prosperity, which ended with the Civil War, an event which was disastrous for all the luxury trades. Small amounts of money from the Dutch Reformed Church in the City enabled the weavers to make tapestries to be sold for a small profit, although the cheaper materials they used meant that the tapestry quality was diminished.

During the Commonwealth period Cromwell made some attempt to revive the business, but the Restoration in 1660 failed to bring the hoped-for resur-

26. *Suthrey House, Mortlake High Street, built early in the seventeenth century as the Upper Dutch House and the only surviving building of the Tapestry Works.*

gence: Charles II preferred paintings to tapestries, and many of the best weavers left Mortlake for factories in Soho and Lambeth. Others left the trade altogether – Philip Hullenberch, for example, stayed on in Mortlake to become the village shoemaker.

On 9 April 1703, the Mortlake works were closed. The buildings were dilapidated and nothing was left inside but a few old patterns and looms. Queen Anne authorised the closure and gave her permission for the buildings to be used for other purposes.

As far as is known, local people were not employed at the works, although many of the second generation of weavers were Mortlake born. Some weavers stayed on to become members of the local community, such as the Hullenberch family which anglicized its name to Hollyberry and Holmbury. Joanna, widow of Jan Hullenberch, the last master weaver at the works, left three small houses in Mortlake to the parish, the rents of which were to benefit the poor.

The Tapestry Works had a lasting effect on the religious life of the parish – the inter-marriage of Dutch Lutherans and local families possibly explains why Mortlake had such a large dissenting congregation in the seventeenth century. In response to the questions posed by the Compton Survey of 1676, the incumbent of the parish church reported "fourscore

dissenters from the Church of England or therea-bouts in this parish, some through ignorance and others through obstinacy refusing to submit to the order and discipline of the said church". In Barnes there were only seven dissenters the same year.

Francis Cleyn's house became a confectioner's shop long before it was demolished in the early 1960s. The Upper Dutch House still stands as the projecting wing of 119 Mortlake High Street. The main tapestry house, the Lower Dutch House, survived until 1951 when it was pulled down by the Borough of Barnes, leaving only the sub-structure and the bricked up watergate. A plaque which had proclaimed its former glory was removed to the council depot, where it disappeared. The site, now a pleasant open space overlooking the river, is marked by an inscribed granite memorial, donated by the South Square Trust, the Barnes and Mortlake History Society and the Mortlake with East Sheen Society. This was unveiled on 25 September 1996 by the Mayor of Richmond upon Thames, Councillor Mike Rowlands.

The true memorial to the weavers is, however, the Mortlake tapestries themselves. Large numbers have survived to grace the walls of palaces, castles, stately homes, museums and private houses throughout the world.

27. A section of the Panorama of the Thames, 1820, published by Samuel Leigh, showing part of the Mortlake riverfront west of the parish church, with the Queen's Head on the extreme left. The marking of the Pottery by the unknown artist is probably incorrect. The low building with a broad kiln or chimney on the far right is almost certainly Sanders' Pottery.

Industrial Enterprises

A survey of 1617 makes no mention of any kind of industry in Mortlake, but in the period from 1619 to 1800, a few small businesses were founded close to the river on the north side of the High Street. All but one were destined to be relatively short-lived, but the earliest known, the Mortlake Tapestry Works (see p26), served to set the scene for the future industrial nature of the Mortlake riverside. The tapestry works was soon joined by a sugar house and by 1703, there were malthouses, which were later followed by two small potteries and two small breweries during that century. Of all these activities, only brewing (see p34) has survived.

SUGAR BOILING AND MALTING

Sugar refining on the Mortlake riverside was carried on in 1688 by William Mucklow, a Quaker at premises between the river and the High Street to the east of Bull's Alley. By 1729 it was in the hands of John Bentley, the last known sugar refiner in Mortlake, but around thirteen years later the sugar house was no longer in use and the building became the first Mortlake Pottery.

Malting was a thriving local industry from the seventeenth until well into the nineteenth century. Together with Nine Elms and Wandsworth, Mortlake was one of the main centres supplying vast quantities of malted grains to the many breweries situated in and around London. In 1811 there were five malthouses and Leigh's *Panorama of the Thames* shows the Mortlake riverside fairly bristling with malthouse cones in 1829. In Barnes a malthouse fronted onto the Terrace with its rear on Back Lane, the surviving section of which was renamed Malthouse Passage in 1890.

THE SANDERS' POTTERY

It is not known why John Sanders, a Lambeth potter, chose Mortlake to start a new manufactory *c*.1743, but perhaps he became aware of the suitability of the site of the disused sugar house: potteries needed substantial volumes of clay for the pots and coal for the kilns – both were heavy and unavailable locally, so that waterborne transport was a basic need.

John Sanders remained active at Lambeth until his death in 1758 and it seems likely that his intention was to have his son William run the Mortlake venture; indeed this is what William did for the next 32 years, and after his death in 1784 the pottery was continued by *his* son John until 1794. Thereafter the

28. One- and two-pint Mortlake Pottery mugs. The one-pint mug, decorated with two continuous bands of foliage has 'F. Winch' impressed on both sides and the date 1837 on the base. The heights are 4¼" and 7¼". 'KISHERE POTTERY MORTLAKE' is impressed on both.

29. Mortlake Pottery hunting jug. Saltglaze stoneware jug with applied decoration of horseman and hounds pursuing a deer, classical scenes, windmills and trees and a large central plaque of Hogarth's 'Modern Midnight Conversation'. The mark 'JK' (for Joseph Kishere) is impressed. Height 8½".

pottery had various owners, but after April 1823 it is listed as empty.

Despite a history extending over 78 years, the wares produced in the Sanders factory are difficult to identify. The type of pottery made was also produced in volume by several other London potteries and, in common with them, Sanders did not mark his wares. Any Sanders' pottery that survives is, therefore, concealed within the large mass of extant London tin-glazed pottery sometimes, and misleadingly, called Delft ware. Evidence of this being made at Mortlake derives from the fact that it was the type of ware produced at Lambeth by John Sanders senior, prior to his setting up the business at Mortlake. Also, an account of the pottery written and published by local historian and solicitor, John Eustace Anderson, in 1894, mentions Delft ware as being among the principal products of the Mortlake Potteries.

Earthenware which was glazed with oxide of tin had an opaque white surface appearance similar to porcelain, but was produced at a fraction of the cost. It required only two firings, one to biscuit stage and another after the glaze and decoration had been applied in a single step. This so-called tin-glazed pottery was produced in Europe over a very long period, but towards the end of the eighteenth century it was displaced by the event of creamware and industrialised processes. Mortimer's *Universal Directory* for 1765 lists William Sanders of Mortlake as a manufacturer of "blue and white and plain white earthenware": the commonest decorative medium used on tin-glazed earthenware was cobalt blue pigment.

During the widening of Mortlake High Street in 1970/1 numerous sherds of blue decorated tin-glazed earthenware were found in the immediate vicinity of the pottery site. A high proportion were from rejected items, but they were sufficient to identify some of the shapes produced by Sanders – small ointment pots, jars, jugs and wine labels, all utilitarian wares of a kind unlikely to have a high survival rate. Archaeological excavation of the actual site has not been possible so a more comprehensive knowledge of the range of wares made at this long-lived pottery may not be attainable.

KISHERE WARE

The second Mortlake Pottery was begun by Joseph Kishere, himself once a worker at the Sanders factory and son of Benjamin Kishere, who was overseer for Sanders. Around 1800, Joseph married a Miss Griffin and, to quote Anderson, "had a little money by her" which together with a win on the state lottery enabled him to begin his own business. This was located on the south side of Mortlake High Street opposite Sanders' pottery, but evidently behind the buildings

30. *Mortlake High Street before 1914, looking west from the parish church. The two gentlemen stand by the entrance to Church Path. St Mary's Wharf was used for the offloading of heavy materials, such as bricks during the property boom of the nineteenth century.*

lining the High Street. Joseph managed the small pottery, seemingly with help from other members of his family, including his son William, who took over at his father's death in 1837.

Only one type of ware was made here, namely saltglaze stoneware, which is a highly-fired impervious earthenware. The glaze is achieved by throwing common salt onto the kiln fires at a particular stage in the firing process. It is a tough, durable pottery with a high survival rate and indeed a good deal of Kishere stoneware does survive, and by good fortune a great deal of it is marked. Marking took the form of impressed lettering on the base of the objects. Often it was 'Kishere Pottery Mortlake Surry [sic]', sometimes 'Kishere' and at other times just 'J.K.' Mortlake is spelt 'Moatlake' more often than seems likely to be due to chance misspelling alone.

Kishere pottery has been described as among the most decorative of the London stonewares. The technique used was the liberal application of plaques which were moulded separately and fused onto the body during firing. The plaques depicted a great variety of scenes among which are Hogarth's Modern Midnight Conversation, classical figures, windmills, trees, cottages, farm implements, drinking (and drunken) scenes and, very frequently on jugs, hunting scenes, giving rise to the term 'hunting jugs'. Horsemen and women are seen riding round the jug with numerous hounds in pursuit of a fox or deer, and some scenes include the kill. Another constant decorative theme was the application of a brown wash of iron oxide applied to the upper part of the wares by a dipping process. Apart from hunting jugs, Kishere's made mugs, lidded tobacco jars, occasional kitchen ware such as colanders, also spittoons, vases and stem cups, sometimes with two handles.

Anderson wrote his account at a time when surviving members of the Kishere family were still living in Mortlake. From them he obtained a number of pieces and also some plaster moulds used to make the plaques applied to the ware. These objects, together with a trade card for Joseph Kishere 'Brown Stone Manufacturer at Mortlake in Surry late Apprentice to Messrs Sanders and Vernon', were presented to the parish church.

Probably the rarest of the Kishere wares was a spirit flask modelled as a hatted sailor figure with a sea bag and anchor at his feet. These figures sometimes carry a name and date on the front. The mould for the figure was among the objects secured by Anderson.

The Mortlake Brewery

While industrialisation of a sort was happening in Mortlake, nothing similar was happening in Barnes, other than the establishment of a brewery there. This is pictured in Leigh's Panorama of c.1820. Dating from the eighteenth century, it belonged first of all to the Hunt family and latterly to the Warings. It was a small concern and most probably its output was intended only to supply the several local inns owned by the Waring family. Demolished by 1840, since 1891 its former site has been occupied by the riverside police station in Lonsdale Road.

MORTLAKE BREWERY

According to the manor court rolls, commercial brewing in Mortlake began during the eighteenth century. The rolls for 1765 mention two small breweries adjacent to each other, but in separate ownership, occupying about two acres. They were on either side of the back lane (Thames Street), a cartway leading to the Town Dock. On the north or river side was the smaller of the two owned by James Weatherstone, an inn-keeper and maltster. On the south side was the larger belonging to William Richmond, a short cut to it being via a narrow alley running down from the High Street, known as Brewhouse Lane. From Thames Street another narrow way named Pembroke Alley ran north towards the river. By 1780 Richmond's brewery had been taken over by John Prior, owner of two local inns and a maltings at Strand on the Green.

In 1807 Weatherstone and an associate named Halford extended his premises northwards to the river by acquiring land with a riverside frontage of 104ft, described as being "an excellent situation for a brewery, maltings or any other building requiring river transport". With this acquisition went Mortlake's last chance of a purely residential riverside.

Weatherstone and Halford took over Prior's business in 1811, and the two small breweries became one. The business passed through various hands until 1852, when the land was sold to 32-year-old Charles John Phillips, who was funded by his father, a coal and corn merchant. A partnership between Phillips and 21-year-old James Wigan, shortly bought out the

31. Waring's Brewery, Barnes, which stood by the river east of the High Street on the site now occupied by the police station. The brewery was demolished before 1840. From an oil painting by J.E. Waring.

32. *Mortlake Brewery, 1893, depicted by W. Luker jnr.*

33. *Mortlake Brewery Wharf, early 1900s, viewed through the legs of the hydraulic crane on the wharf.*

whole business. At that time the brewery was half way down the list of London breweries for output, using around 5,000 quarters of malt per annum as against Barclay's 108,000 quarters.

The next ten years were spent buying up property on adjacent sites – Phillips also bought two local inns, the Ship and the Bull. Prosperity came to the firm via lucrative government contracts for supplying beer to the British army in India (India Pale Ale), and possibly to troops in the Crimean War. By then the brewery was the largest employer of labour in the district, but lack of space was becoming a problem and a drawback was that Thames Street, ran through the heart of it: the street was the only public cartway to the river, with cottages and businesses on either side. The problem was overcome in 1865 by Phillips' acquisition of the freehold of all the land on the riverside for £2,350, and he then proceeded to close off the smaller rights of way to the towpath. The closure of Pembroke Alley prior to the purchase of the freehold met with little resistance, but the initial attempts to close Thames Street and Brewhouse Lane were met by loud public protests. A prolonged and bitter battle between the brewers and the people of Mortlake ended in victory for the brewers. Phillips' promise to widen Bull's Alley into a cartway (and to contribute £200 to the parish poor fund) swayed Mortlake Vestry in his favour and the closure went ahead.

In 1865, a tithe barn, a docking house, a shop with stable, a slaughterhouse, lofts and a blacksmith's workshop were bought jointly by the partners and demolished. The new brewery included a long, high brick wall fronting Mortlake High Street on which the initials P & W were carved into stone roundels beside the legend 'Mortlake Brewery, 1869'. They can be seen on the same wall today.

A misunderstanding between Phillips and Wigan would seem to be behind the ending of the partnership in 1877. Phillips remained as the sole owner and Wigan bought Hawkes' Brewery at Bishops Stortford, though he continued to live in Mortlake. He had a wife and thirteen children, and Phillips had a wife and a family of eight: the families could hardly avoid bumping into each other from time to time and there must have been many awkward moments, especially since the wives appear to have vied with each other for the title of leading society hostess and charity worker in Mortlake. Two of Phillips' sons had reached the age of 21 in 1877, and this may have contributed to the break-up of the partnership. With Wigan gone, Phillips' sons joined what was now the family business and when their father retired in 1889 they sold out to Watney's, staying on as directors. A takeover by Watney's in 1898 resulted in the firm becoming Watney, Combe, Reid and Co. Charles Phillips died in 1901, leaving £100,000.

34. *The new Stag Brewery overshadowing the old houses on Thames Bank. On the left is the Ship Inn, next to it, with a tall tiled roof, is a seventeenth-century house formerly church property and the Star & Garter inn until c.1790. On the far right is Leyden House, the oldest house in Mortlake, which assumed its present form in the eighteenth century, but parts at the rear date back to the sixteenth.*

The history of the brewery since the turn of the century can be seen on the ground. The first move westward was in 1903, when an eight-storey maltings was erected by the riverside on the eastern corner of Ship Lane. When malting ceased the building became offices, but it has been out of use since 1954.

During the 1960s the firm maintained its role as leading local employer with 1,400 on the payroll. Further expansion westward in the early 1970s took the brewery west of Ship Lane between the Lower Richmond Road and Thames Bank, destroying several small alleyways, streets and a paddock in the process. A move across the High Street saw the erection of offices which have since been vacated. Expansion did not mean more jobs – use of modern technology brought a steady decline in the workforce, so that by 1986 the total number was 400, including

management and office personnel.

Recently the brewery has changed hands once again, the present owners being the Stag Brewing Co. Ltd. Extensive demolition and rebuilding has taken place and some fairly modern buildings have been replaced by those of a more traditional style. The maltings, with listed building status, stay on as a riverside landmark and the facade of the 1869 building is preserved. A bottling plant for a well-known brand of lager is being sited to the east of Ship Lane, while lager brewing will occupy the western half of the site. The new owners have taken care to consult with local people, and Mortlake looks with interest on this latest phase in the life of its best-known local industry.

35. *Watney's Mortlake Brewery and Thames Bank, 1965. The brewery was developed on the site between Ship Lane and Bull's Alley from the mid-1860s. Considerable alterations were made after the last war, but it has now been replaced by a new brewery west of Ship Lane behind Thames Bank. Of the buildings in this photograph only the imposing malthouse of 1903 still stands, though malting ceased in 1954.*

Rural Retreats

Members of the gentry and City merchant class began to settle in the area in the seventeenth century. The beauty of the upper slopes of East Sheen in particular proved attractive to the would-be small country estate owners who needed to stay in touch with the City. Typical of these was a member of a wealthy Brabant family, Abraham Cullen, a City merchant connected with the wool trade. In 1655 he came to live in the former manor house of East Sheen and Westhall. Another was Edward Colston, Bristol merchant and philanthropist, who preferred the riverside ambience of Mortlake village. His business frequently took him to London and in 1689 he acquired the lease of Cromwell House, Thames Bank as a convenient residence. In his spare time he tended his lovely garden or watched the river from a gazebo set in the wall. The house was pulled down in 1854 and replaced with another of the same name, closer to the river with a garden at the rear. The new Cromwell House, home of the brewer James Wigan, was demolished in 1947 and a third Cromwell House built, but the gates of the very first house are preserved in Williams Lane, off the Lower Richmond Road.

THE KIT-CAT CLUB

Just to the north of the manor house at Barn Elms was a smaller house, long known as Queen Elizabeth's Dairy. In 1703 its tenant was Jacob Tonson, stationer, publisher and secretary to the Kit-Cat Club, whose members included Steele, Addison, Marlborough, Robert Walpole, Congreve, Vanbrugh and Kneller – some of the leading Whigs of the day. Ostensibly the club's rôle was to encourage literature and the fine arts, but its true purpose was to promote the House of Hanover and the Protestant Succession. Horace Walpole was to refer to the members as "the patriots who saved Britain". In London, the club met at the Fountain Tavern, owned by Christopher Cat, whose mutton pies, known as Kit-Cats, gave the club its name. Tonson acquired the house at Barn Elms as a secluded retreat away from London, where members could meet: a room was designed by him especially for this purpose.

Sir Godfrey Kneller was commissioned to paint portraits of the members, which they gave to Tonson. These and the lease of the house were left to his nephew, also Jacob, and in 1733 he commissioned Henry Joynes to design a building in the Palladian style to house the 48 pictures. Over the chimney were portraits of the Duke of Newcastle and the Earl of Lincoln, and the rest were hung in three rows of ten, and a fourth row containing sixteen. They were there until 1772 when the Tonson connection with Barn Elms ended, and in 1945 they were acquired for the

36. *Jacob Tonson (1656-1736), publisher and secretary of the Kit-Cat Club, who leased Barn Elms.*

nation and are now in the collection of the National Portrait Gallery. Tonson's house and the new building were demolished early in the nineteenth century and the grounds incorporated into those of the manor house.

THE HOARE FAMILY AT BARN ELMS

The Hoare family took up occupation of the manor house, Barn Elms, in the eighteenth century. Sir Richard Hoare, head of the banking family which operated from Fleet Street, was Lord Mayor of London in 1745. His son, also Richard, was born at Barn Elms and when he inherited the property did much to improve it. In 1772 two wings were added to the house, and two Gothic lodges built on the carriage approach from Putney. The formal canal to the west of the house was enlarged to create an ornamental lake of four acres with winding banks, grotto, island and footbridge. Throughout the occupation of the Hoare family, links were forged with the local people.

The last member of the family at Barn Elms was Henry Hugh Hoare. He declined to allow the Hammersmith Bridge Company to build access roads to the bridge across his land, and the company had little option but to buy the entire estate. Inevitably

37. *Barn Elms in the 1840s, when the house was occupied by Sir Lancelot Shadwell, Vice-Chancellor of England. From a steel engraving after Thomas Allom.*

38. *Elm Grove, Barnes, 1837. This house stood on the site of Elm Grove Road at the junction with Rocks Lane with grounds extending to Barnes Common. It was demolished c.1897. From a coloured lithograph by Laura Jones.*

it was then broken up, although the manor house remained, complete with 120 acres of land.

A large house on the Barn Elms Estate was Elm Grove. This stood close to Church Road, its grounds extending to the Common, with Beverley Brook running through them, and with a cottage and two coach houses on the estate with servants' quarters. From 1826 to 1860 the house was occupied by Baron Alexandre de Sampayo, attaché to the Portuguese Embassy. It was demolished c.1896, but gave its name to Elm Grove Road.

VILLAS AND MANSIONS IN BARNES VILLAGE

A number of large houses were built in Barnes in the eighteenth century. One, The Cedars, was built on an enclosure from the Common in c.1780, and others stood in their own grounds on Barnes Green. One of these was The Laurels. Built about 1705, it was the property of John Nightingale, a Lombard Street banker. From 1802-1816 it was leased to Sir Henry Halford, President of the College of Physicians and physician to George IV, William IV and Queen Victoria, who used the house as a country retreat. It later became Henry Hoare's last home in Barnes. When he sold the property in 1845 there were stables, a coach house, a brick granary, a garden house, melon pits and a hot house on its 22 acres of grounds. The last private tenant was Henry Alexander, a solicitor with financial interests in the development of South Kensington (his son William gave £80,000 to build the National Portrait Gallery). In 1885 most of the

grounds were sold for building development, the house becoming a boys' school before its demolition in c.1930.

Elegant villas also appeared alongside the small cottages by the Barnes riverside, which became known as The Terrace. They were especially popular as summer lets, and among the residents in 1818 were Mr and Mrs Papendiek at no. 7, who were court musician and lady-in-waiting respectively to George III and Queen Caroline at Kew Palace. Their daughter and son-in-law Joseph Planta, diplomat and secretary to Canning and Castlereagh, were living at Milbourne House in 1818.

No. 27 The Terrace was the scene of a gruesome double murder and suicide. The murder victims were the Count and Countess d'Antraigues, a French couple who had spent their lives embroiled in political intrigue in Europe before coming to Barnes. On 22 July 1812, they were murdered by their Italian servant, Lorenzo, who then committed suicide and was later buried at the Mill Hill crossroads. A letter to *The Times* soon after complained that Lorenzo's grave was being opened up so that passers-by, including the d'Antraigues funeral party, might view the body.

Two large mansions on The Terrace were Elm Bank (c.1760) and St Ann's. The latter was built by Nathan Spriggs, a wealthy Jamaica merchant, c.1765. It stood east of the Bull's Head in a commanding position, set apart from the main Terrace, with grounds that stretched some distance along what is now Lonsdale

39. (Left) The Laurels, a Georgian house which stood on the east side of Barnes Green. It became Beverley Boys' School in its later years, before its demolition c.1930.

40. (Right) Milbourne House in Station Road opposite the Pond, the oldest surviving house in Barnes. It assumed its present form in the eighteenth century, but the main structure is probably sixteenth century. Only a public outcry prevented its demolition in 1945. Drawing by Hanslip Fletcher, 1946.

41. St Ann's in the late 1890s. This eighteenth-century house stood by the river on the site now occupied by St Ann's and Lyric Roads, and was one of the most important in Barnes. It was the home for some years of William, 2nd Earl of Lonsdale. In its last years it was the headquarters of the Lyric Club.

Road and as far as the High Street, where the main carriage entrance was situated. (This is now the entrance to a car repair business.) Residents included William Lowther, 2nd Earl of Lonsdale, who bought the house in 1846 and retained it until his death in 1872, in the meantime entertaining guests lavishly. To add to the country atmosphere, Lonsdale retained the farm and market gardens which occupied most of the land. The house ended its life as the country branch of a London club, The Lyric. It was demolished about 1900 and in 1903, St Ann's Road and Lyric Road were built on the grounds.

DESIRABLE RESIDENCES IN MORTLAKE

In the eighteenth century, a number of large houses stood facing Mortlake High Street at its eastern end, with gardens running down to the river. Largest and most imposing of the survivors is The Limes, built about 1720, whose grounds included a field on the south side of the High Street containing a fine avenue of limes. Past residents have included a distinguished Jewish family of merchants and bankers, the Franks (1754 to 1803), the unfortunate Lady Byron, and from

1880-83, Quintin Hogg, founder of the polytechnic movement. In the 1820s, J.M.W. Turner painted two well-known pictures of the house and riverside terrace, while staying with his friend Mr Moffatt.

Portobello House stood on the south side of South Worple Way It was built *c*.1750 by Vice-Admiral Perry Mayne (1700-61), who took part in the reduction of Porto Bello in 1738 and named his house after that battle. In 1775 it became the home of a Roman Catholic family named Gandolphi, who were there until 1841. After them came Lady Constantia Mostyn, also a Catholic. During her occupation, the Religious Census of 1851 for Mortlake recorded a chapel over the hayloft as being used by a Roman Catholic congregation of 140 seated and 50-60 standing. The house was demolished in 1893.

The surviving large houses near the Mortlake riverside are witness to a fashionable period in the eighteenth century, but the smell from malting and brewing, not to mention the dung-barges, plus toxic fumes from the saltglazed pottery, can hardly have been conducive to country living. East Sheen was definitely the place to be.

42. *The Limes (now 123 Mortlake High Street) and its gardens as pictured by J.M.W. Turner in 1827. The house was built c.1720 and served as the council offices from 1895-1940 when it was damaged by bombing. After restoration the house has continued in use as commercial offices. The gardens extended along the river, but have been entirely built over.*

43. *Portobello House, Mortlake. Built c.1740, occupying extensive grounds south of the Worple Way. Demolished in 1893, Vernon, Howgate and Oaklands Roads now occupy the site.*

A PLACE OF HIGH AND SECRET WALLS

A.C. Benson described East Sheen as "a place of high and secret walls with great trees and solid facades within". One of these properties was a seventeenth-century house later known as Temple Grove, which was once the manor house of East Sheen and Westhall. Sir John Temple, Speaker and Attorney General to the Irish Parliament, bought it as a retirement home, and died there in 1704, but the Temple family held the house for many years and succeeding generations enlarged the house and estate. In 1723, Henry Temple became the first Viscount Palmerston and his grandson became the famous Prime Minister, but at *his* coming of age the estates in East Sheen were sold. Later the house became a renowned boys' preparatory school. It was demolished at the turn of the century.

Not so far from the Green, in Sheen Lane, stood another house called The Cedars, for many years the home of Sir Brook Watson, Lord Mayor of London, who had a distinguished career in the City. As a boy he lost a leg to a shark in Havana harbour, an event recorded in a grisly painting by John Singleton Copley, which is said to have been hung in the dining room. Later, the house became the home of a well-known local family, the Leycester-Penrhyns. Edward Leycester-Penrhyn was the first Chairman of Surrey County Council from 1889. The house survived until 1930.

On the opposite side of Sheen Lane was Sheen House. Rebuilt in 1786, it was one of the finest houses in East Sheen. Among its residents was Henry Hope, a banker from Amsterdam, and the Marquis of Ailesbury who let the house to Earl Grey, the Prime Minister, in 1831 – important meetings concerning the Reform Bill were held there. Next came Joshua Bates, a director of Baring's merchant bank, who provided a temporary home for members of the French royal family after the abdication of Louis Philippe in 1848. A further French connection was the exiled heir to the French throne and his wife, the Comte and Comtesse de Paris. They leased the house in 1886 and celebrated their silver wedding there in 1889 with a party for 500 guests led by the Prince and Princess of Wales. The Comte and Comtesse were the last private residents. The house later became a Club and was demolished in 1907.

In the early eighteenth century several houses were built on the old common fields. Palewell Lodge was on Stonehill Shott, north of Palewell Common, and East Sheen Lodge was on Little Whittings Shott, west of Sheen Lane. The latter had a succession of illustrious occupants ranging from Alderman John Barber, Lord Mayor of London, Sir Phillip Francis, reputed

44. Temple Grove, c.1812, a house which dated back to at least the early seventeenth century and one of the most important in East Sheen. The home of the Temple family for some years, but in 1811 became the Temple Grove Preparatory School. It was demolished when the school moved to Eastbourne in 1908. The entrance was in Sheen Lane. Palmerston and Observatory Roads cover its grounds. Engraving from a drawing by J.E. Neale.

45. *The Cedars on the west side of Sheen Lane. The photograph shows a garden party in its grounds not long before its demolition in 1930. Cedar Court flats occupy the site of the house and the Cedar Parade of shops in the Upper Richmond Road part of the grounds.*

46. *East Sheen Lodge, an eighteenth-century house on the west side of Sheen Lane, with grounds extending to Richmond Park. Its residents included the 1st Duke of Fife who married Princess Louise in 1889. It was by a pond in the garden that her brother, the future King George V, proposed to Queen Mary. Lithograph by T. Way.*

47. Sir Brook Watson (1735-1807), who lived at The Cedars, East Sheen from 1780. He was Lord Mayor in 1796. Caricature by R. Dighton jnr, 1803.

48. Sir Philip Francis (1740-1818), civil servant in India and bitter enemy of Warren Hastings. He lived at East Sheen Lodge 1783-1805, and was buried in Mortlake parish church. Portrait by J. Lonsdale.

49. Sheen House, which fronted the east side of Sheen Lane. It was built for Charles Bowles on the site of an earlier house, possibly designed by John Carr. It was demolished c.1907 and Muirdown and Shrewsbury Avenues and Richmond Park Road are laid out on its grounds.

author of the 'Letters of Junius', and in 1880, the Duke of Fife, who married Princess Louise, daughter of Edward VII.   In the garden on 2 May 1893, Princess May of Teck became engaged to the Duke of York – the couple were later George V and Queen Mary. The grounds were built over in 1926, but the house survived until 1965.

To the west of East Sheen Lodge is Percy Lodge. Threatened with demolition in 1926, it was rescued by architect, Robert Atkinson, who restored it for his own use and designed the houses built on the grounds.

WHITE LODGE

Mortlake can boast a royal residence – White Lodge may be in Richmond Park, but it is in the parish of Mortlake. Begun by George I as a hunting lodge, it was completed by George II in 1729. George III and

50. *Palewell Lodge, 1893. The Palewell estate was the largest in East Sheen and its sale in 1896 heralded the development of the area. The Lodge was demolished in 1925 and All Saints' Church stands near its site. Drawing by Albert Betts.*

51. *Percy Lodge, Christ Church Road. Built c.1740 and the only eighteenth century house that survives in East Sheen.*

52. *Henry Addington, 1st Viscount Sidmouth (1757-1844).
He lived at White Lodge while he was Prime Minister.*

53. *White Lodge, Richmond Park. The seldom illustrated east
front of this fine mansion in Mortlake. The main block was
built in 1727-29, probably to the designs of Roger Morris.
Wings were added some years later and the portico and front
corridors in the early nineteenth century.*

54. *Sir Edwin Chadwick (1800-90) (left) with Dr. B.W.
Richardson (standing) and Professor Sir Richard Owen.*

Queen Caroline used it as an occasional residence
and in 1801 the King gave it to his Prime Minister,
Henry Addington (later Viscount Sidmouth), who
lived there until his death in 1844. Queen Victoria
retained the house in her own hands from 1857 and
used it from time to time. Local traders felt the benefit
of her tenure. Seal the butcher in Barnes High Street,
and Phillips and Wigan, the Mortlake brewers, had
royal appointment warrants, while Falla's long established hardware and oil shop in Mortlake High
Street supplied hearthstones, scrubbing brushes,
housemaids' gloves, best mops and yards of flannel
to "Her Majesty, White Lodge". Falla's account books,

lodged at Surrey Record Office, record the patronage
of many wealthy residents of Mortlake and Barnes.
In 1869 the Lodge became the home of the Duke and
Duchess of Teck. Their daughter, Princess May, lived
there until her marriage to the future King George
V, returning there for the birth of the Prince who
became Edward VIII – the bells of Mortlake Church
were the first to announce the event; the baptism
was held at White Lodge in the presence of Queen
Victoria. The future George VI and Queen Elizabeth
spent some time there after their marriage in 1923.
Since 1955 White Lodge has been the home of the
Royal Ballet School.

Another Mortlake house in the Park was Sheen
Cottage, east of Sheen Gate. Built by Walpole for his
huntsman, from 1852 it was the home of Professor
Richard Owen, naturalist and first Director of the
Natural History Museum. The garden of the cottage
lay outside the Park, adjoining that of Owen's great
friend, Sir Edwin Chadwick, who lived in retirement
at Park Cottage from 1869 until his death in 1890.
Chadwick, irascible senior civil servant, shaper of the
New Poor Law of 1834 and fanatical sanitary reformer, was reviled and hated by the establishment,
but to his friend Owen he was "my dear old Chaddy".
Sheen Cottage was badly damaged in World War II
and never rebuilt, but Chadwick's old home managed to outlive many of the grander houses in the
area: it was demolished in 1932.

55. *Castelnau House, Mortlake. An eighteenth-century house which stood by the river opposite Ashleigh Road. It was the home of the Boileau family for a century, and latterly a school for young ladies before demolition by the council in 1907. Watercolour by an unknown artist.*

Villages into Suburbs

BUILDING IN NORTH BARNES

Though many of the changes in Barnes followed the opening of the railway station in 1846, significant developments had already occurred in North Barnes to coincide with the opening of the new Hammersmith Bridge. About 1826 the approach roads were being laid out. Upper Bridge Road (Castelnau) ran south from the bridge to join a former track, Rocks Lane, to link with Roehampton. An earlier plan by the Hammersmith Bridge Company to run the road across Barnes Pond was rejected. Lower Bridge Road (Lonsdale Road) followed the course of the river, skirting land purchased by the West Middlesex Water Company for reservoirs, to join Barnes Terrace. (The four Barn Elms reservoirs were built to the east of Castelnau in 1894.) Housing development began *c.*1840, with large dignified houses at the bridge end of Lonsdale Road, and then from 1842 'carriage class'

villas were built along Castelnau, together with a pub, the Boileau Arms.   By 1866, there were 140 houses and 800 people living in the immediate area, almost as many as the entire population of Barnes in 1801. The original developer was Major Charles Boileau of Mortlake, whose ancestral home in France was called Castelnau.

Development was not entirely middle class however, for in 1858 Cowan's Soap and Candle Works and sugar refinery was built to the east of Castelnau, near to the bridge. Though an intrusion in social terms, it did provide a good source of employment for the working classes in Barnes until a disastrous fire in 1888 led to the factory's closure in 1892 and the loss of 500 jobs. Harrods Depository was built on its site.

Mansion flats were built in roads on the east side of Castelnau close to the bridge from about 1910, and by 1922 the area of North Barnes had a population of 3,460. This was doubled with the building of the cottage-style Castelnau Estate by the London County Council in 1926 on the site of Harold Bessent's market garden. The 640 ferro-concrete cottages, built by

56. Castelnau Mansions, by Hammersmith Bridge.

57. Castelnau Villas 1842, the first houses to be built in Castelnau, designed by Henry Loxton. The villas are now Nos. 84-122 and 91-125 Castelnau. From a watercolour in the Paton Collection.

58. Castelnau Estate, Barnes. The 'Boot' houses under construction 1927.

Henry Boot & Sons by a method known as the Boot Pier and Panel System, were part of a scheme to ease overcrowded conditions in Fulham and Hammersmith. Tenants were particularly happy with their gardens which, unsurprisingly, yielded generous crops. This pleasant, well laid out estate was bought from the GLC by Richmond upon Thames Council in 1971, and during the late 70s many tenants purchased their homes under the 'right-to-buy' scheme.

THE WESTFIELDS

In the Westfields area (the final 's' is a nineteenth-century addition), the railway ran across market garden land, the freehold of which was bought in 1865 by Walter Whittingham of the British Land Company for £1296. In sharp contrast to the spacious residences of North Barnes, streets of cheap terraced cottages were laid out, corner shops and beerhouses sprang up and small shopping parades appeared in White Hart Lane. By the turn of the century, the overcrowded cottages teemed with life and there was much poverty: difficult to envisage today, when the cottages are privately owned, with colourful gardens and all modern facilities.

59. A corner shop in Westfields, 1977.

60. *View from the railway of Westfields in 1961, showing Railway Side and the allotments with the Bee Hive public house and Westfields school.*

A PLACE FOR COMMUTERS

After Barnes Station was built on the Common, houses within easy walking distance were snapped up by City commuters. The four early nineteenth-century houses and three cottages on the former Mill enclosure on the Common, advertised as being only three minutes' walk from the station "bringing London, by that route, within twenty minutes ride", were swiftly sold at auction in 1858.

New houses in Scarth, Station, Beverley, Woodlands and Cleveland Roads were in great demand. In 1894 most of the land belonging to The Cedars went to make Cedars Road, where the houses built between 1896 and 1901 were said to be "close to the Green, the common and the Railway Station". Not far away across the Green, houses adorned with small sandstone lions were built on the former grounds of Hillersdon House and The Laurels from *c*.1899 – the 'Lion houses' are now a well-known feature of Barnes. More shops were opened in the High Street and Church Road and the 1901 census showed that the population of Barnes was just below 10,000.

Further development took place between the wars, including the high quality houses on the Lowther Estate where road names are either associated with the Lonsdale properties (Cumberland, Westmoreland, Suffolk), or the family's diplomatic postings (Washington, Madrid, Galata and Belgrave). In the early

1920s, the squalid cottages huddled behind Barnes Terrace were demolished and replaced by Terrace Gardens and Limes Avenue, the first council housing in Barnes. Since World War II, new local authority housing has been small or medium sized blocks of flats – none is high rise.

In spite of the changes central Barnes with its church, the Green, duck pond, small shops and a sprinkling of older houses is still something of a village – estate agents often refer to it as such.

CHANGE AT EAST SHEEN

The first post-railway developments in East Sheen were on farmland stretching from Upper Richmond Road to the farmhouse near the entrance to Sheen Common. Derby and Stanley Roads were constructed on the lower slopes, and the roads later to be known as Temple Sheen on the land near the Common. Thomas Hare, political reformer, built the first house, Sheen Mount, in 1853, and the next was Uplands overlooking the Common. In Fife Road the architect Arthur Blomfield designed his own house, The Cottage, and also The Halsteads, notable for being one of the first houses to be built of concrete, in 1868. Another leading architect, T.E. Colcutt designed Oakdene in Christchurch Road.

On the east side of Sheen Lane, Stonehill and Vic-

61. *The river end of Barnes High Street c.1910.*

62. *The development of Edwardian Barnes. Madrid Road c.1910. The paths and road are not made up and in the distance the site of the future Castelnau Estate is still market gardens.*

63. *Clare Lawn. The largest and grandest of East Sheen's Victorian houses, although it stood for only sixty years. Built in 1866 for (Sir) Frederick Wigan on an eleven-acre site bordering Richmond Park on the east side of Sheen Lane. The house was extended in 1893, but was demolished c.1926 and Clare Lawn Avenue laid out on the site. The photograph of the front comes from the final sale particulars.*

64. *One of the most extraordinary of the Victorian houses of East Sheen, Sheen Mount. Built in 1852 for Thomas Hare who designed it himself. Its gardens were a favourite venue for fêtes. Demolished after the last war and Sheen Mount Primary School built on its site.*

arage Roads were laid out and the earliest houses built, the Vicarage in 1866 and three houses in Stonehill Road designed by Ingress Bell – The Grange, Hinxton House and Stonehill. Bell was a leading architect and said to be the best draughtsman of his day. The finest and largest of these Victorian houses in East Sheen was built in 1866 for Frederick Wigan, a Southwark hop merchant, brother of James Wigan the brewer (see p.36). This was Clare Lawn, which stood in eleven acres of ground with eight reception rooms, twenty bed and dressing rooms and numerous bathrooms. It was in fine condition when it was demolished in 1926.

Intensive suburban development began in 1896 with the sale of fifty acres of the Palewell estate. East Sheen, Gilpin and Park Avenues were laid out over a wide area of meadowland, along with the first shopping parade in the Upper Richmond Road. Other estates were sold before the First World War: Spencer House, (Martindale and Spencer Gardens), The Firs (Sheen Gate Gardens and Firs Avenue), Sheen House (Richmond Park Road, Muirdown and Shrewsbury Avenues) and Temple Grove (Palmerston, Observatory and Percival Roads). Except for the Sheen House estate, all had been built over by 1914.

Building resumed after 1918. The Sheen House estate, Park Cottage, Clare Lawn and the grounds of East Sheen Lodge all went for development. Wayside replaced The Angles, and The Mall appeared in the grounds of Percy Lodge. In 1931, shops in the Upper Richmond Road, Penrhyn Crescent and Colston Road replaced The Cedars. Between 1932 and 1939 the remaining land south of the Upper Richmond Road

65. The Frederick Wigan Institute, later the Wigan Hall. Built in 1890 in North Worple Way near the station, it served as a the parish meeting hall from 1910 until 1969. Demolished 1972.

66. Shops in the Upper Richmond Road, with the trees marking the site of Milton Road. Note the Royal Arms.

67. *Shops in the Upper Richmond Road in the 1920s, looking towards Putney. It was the building of these shops before and after the First World War that led to the eclipse of Mortlake High Street as the area's main shopping centre. Philip Davies was a well-known local firm that traded until 1971.*

68. *Upper Richmond Road in the 1930s after the demolition of The Cedars and the widening of the road. Of Milestone Green only the milestone remains.*

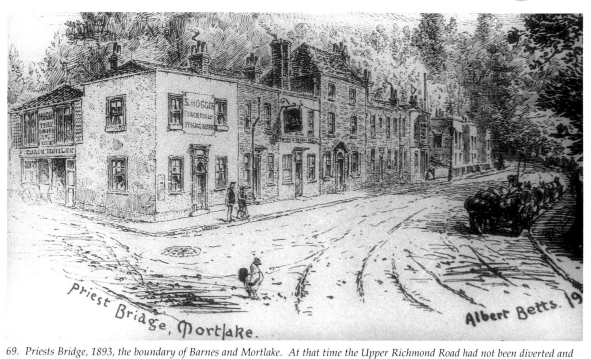

69. Priests Bridge, 1893, the boundary of Barnes and Mortlake. At that time the Upper Richmond Road had not been diverted and Priests Bridge was the main road. Known also as Hogger's Corner, from the wheelwright business on the corner, next to the Market Gardener Inn. Drawing by Albert Betts.

70. The river at the end of Ship Lane, with the Ship and Thames Bank c.1900. The timber building and wall on the left were demolished a few years later to make way for the large malthouse which still stands.

71. *Mortlake High Street c.1900. The bollards and the young girl stand at the entrance ot Church Path.*

72. Wrights Walk between Mortlake High Street and the railway. The pair nearest the camera date from 1850, the further pair c.1860, and closely resemble Model Cottages. They were of a very high standard for the period. Photographed in 1964 before being modernised and extended.

had been taken and the estates, market gardens and orchards which had characterised the area for so long had completely disappeared. East Sheen had become a suburb of London

MORTLAKE AFTER THE RAILWAY

In Mortlake development began soon after the railway opened in 1846. The line ran down the middle of the Worple Way, a headland which formerly lay between the commonfields.

Between the railway and the north side of the Upper Richmond Road, the tiny Nelson Cottages in Sheen Lane pre-dated the opening by one year. When they were built they had minute front gardens, but even these disappeared with road widening. Most of the shops in Sheen Lane today date from between 1895 and 1910.

In 1851, substantial houses for middle-class commuters were built on the north side of St Leonard's Road. Next came Model Cottages, a small estate lying between St Leonard's Road and the Upper Richmond Road, the work of two public benefactors, intended for working class families: those on the east side were built by the Labourers' Friend Society between 1852 and 1858, and those on the west by E.H. Leycester-Penrhyn of The Cedars, Sheen Lane, between 1862 and 1870. Today, this delightful rural backwater is much sought after by those who were certainly not in the minds of the original planners. Further development of the area to the west of Sheen Lane was delayed until the turn of the century. The Ormonde Road/Leinster Avenue area was built c.1905.

To the west of Clifford Avenue, the roads between Tangier Road and the Upper Richmond Road were

73. *Much of the land east of Mortlake parish church was open fields until the early part of this century. These allotments are on the site of Ripley Gardens, with the backs of the houses in the High Street and the bus garage in Avondale Road and Tinderbox Alley on the right.*

74. *A Mortlake High Street shop, Leach Brothers, and its staff. Despite its well-stocked windows, the store was soon to close, being demolished to make way for the first, and only, Mortlake cinema in 1913.*

75. *Mortlake High Street c.1920, looking east from the brewery. The shop next to Arthur Jarrett, with an eighteenth-century frontage, is the oil and hardware shop of Arthur Falla, one of the best-known of Mortlake businesses. Note the Old George and the Two Brewers beyond.*

76. *An Edwardian view of Mortlake High Street with the brewery in the background. The houses next to the Lord Napier dated back at least to the 17th-18th centuries, but were demolished after the Second World War. The Victorian row next to them is being incorporated in a new development at the time of writing.*

77. *Mortlake High Street in the early 1900s, showing the new Electricity works and The Limes before the development of the fields between Avondale Road and White Hart Lane. The Limes took its name from an avenue of lime trees which formed the approach to the house from the south and was, from 1895-1940, the Council Offices.*

built on the former market gardens of the Barker family in the mid-1920s. Between the railway and the river, Council housing was built in the Langdon Place and Lambert Avenue area by the end of the 1920s. East of Clifford Avenue to the south of the railway, St Leonard's Court, Eastbourne Gardens and The Byeway were developments of the 1930s.

To the east of Sheen Lane, between the railway and the north side of the Upper Richmond Road, Queen's Road was the first to be built in 1850. Development continued westward to Alexandra Road, where the first council houses in Mortlake were built in 1896, and by 1908, housing had reached as far as Sheen Lane.

Behind the south side of Mortlake High Street, between Sheen Lane and Church Path, the cottages in Wright's Walk were built 1850-70, following the medieval strips in Ewe Furlong. E.H. Leycester

Penrhyn and Sir Frederick Wigan provided cheap rentable housing in nearby Victoria Road. East of the parish church towards White Hart Lane, Ashleigh, Avondale and Cowley Roads and First and Second Avenues were laid out with a mixture of houses and flats built between 1903-6, much favoured by employees at the newly-built bus garage in Avondale Road. The earliest block of council flats in the High Street was Avondale House, built in 1932; another council development was Chertsey Court, built to house people from the run-down area behind the old Bull Inn, many of whom had worked on the site of their new home when it was Clifford's market garden. Supermarket car parks and the Sheen Lane Centre cover the site of their old homes.

In 1901 the population of Mortlake with East Sheen was over 10,000; by 1991 there were around 22,854 people living in 10,527 dwellings.

78. *Avondale Road c.1914. The bus garage on the left was built in 1901 as stables for horse buses. Motor buses arrived in 1906.*

79. *Of the Victorian houses and cottages in Mortlake, this pair in Victoria Road are among the most unusual. Built of concrete in 1875, they are among the oldest concrete buildings in the country.*

Civic Changes

Local government changes inevitably resulted from an increasing population. Parish vestries, which had held sway since the reign of Elizabeth I, were no longer adequate administrative bodies for the problems that many more people brought. Also, they had neither the powers, nor the popular support which were desirable in the nineteenth century.

Vestries were managed by those ratepayers who paid the highest rates. In *Mortlake Memories*, John Eustace Anderson, clerk to the Mortlake Vestry, tells how before the railway came "there being few gentlemen residing in Mortlake", the gentry from East Sheen ruled the parish, and that vestry meetings were controlled by "eight or ten gentlemen sitting round a table in the middle of the room", while tradesmen, who relied on their patronage, sat on forms round the sides twiddling their hats. Only the market gardeners, who opposed most innovations such as sewers, could afford to be independent. The vestry minutes for Barnes reveal a similar oligarchy but, noted Anderson, when the railway came the people who lived there did not then have to depend on the village for their livelihood.

80. Graph showing the population growth between 1801 and 1901, compared with the totals in 1991.

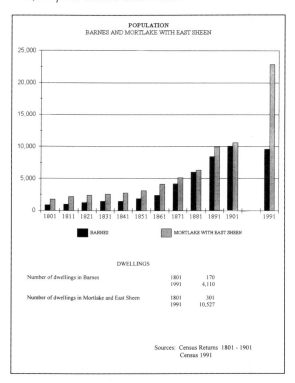

81. The Barnes Fire Brigade proudly parading its new mechanised fire engines outside the fire station alongside The Limes, 1913.

82. *Charter Day, 14 September 1932. The Charter Mayor, Cllr J.P. Firmston, receiving the Charter from the Lord-Lieutenant in a ceremony on Barnes Common.*

However well intentioned, vestries were unable to cope with the problems of urbanisation. Their powers were gradually eroded by boards set up with government approval to deal with such matters as highways, sewerage, drains, housing and health, usually, it must be said, with the agreement of the vestrymen themselves. Government legislation which encouraged improvements in such fields was, however, usually permissive and the vestries were not obliged to do anything. An example of this was the matter of street lighting. In 1849, Mortlake Vestry arranged for the Richmond and Brentford Gas Companies to lay mains for street lighting, but in fact the streets remained unlit until 1860, largely due to the opposition of the market gardeners who feared a rise in rates. The gardeners also delayed the arrival of tap water, but around the middle of the century mains for domestic supplies were laid by the West Middlesex Water Works.

Strong opposition, mainly from Barnes, failed to prevent the union of the parishes of Barnes and Mortlake with East Sheen in March 1893, when they became the Barnes District Board: as one local his-

torian put it, long term differences between the two parishes meant that they were reluctant to become engaged, let alone married. Remnants of the vestries disappeared completely when the Urban District Council of Barnes was formed in 1894. The new Council held its first meeting on 31 December 1894, and in 1895 The Limes in Mortlake High Street became the Council Office; here too there was wharfage and space for a council depot and from 1898 the Fire Brigade was stationed there as well. There was also space for the Council to set up its own electricity works, which opened on 1 May, 1901 – it produced the cheapest electricity in the country for many years.

In November 1926, the Council decided to seek incorporation as a municipal borough, but it was not until 12 September, 1932 that an incorporation ceremony took place in a marquee opposite the Gate House on Barnes Common. Here the mayor, John Firmston, accepted the Charter of Incorporation and, amid scenes of jubilation, the Borough of Barnes was established. So began an important phase in local government which ended on 1 April 1965.

83. The final meeting of Barnes Council in the Penrhyn Rooms at the Bull, East Sheen on 10 March, 1965. The Mayor was Cllr A.G.H. Lawrence and on his left the Mayor's chaplain was the Rev. Samuel Erskine, Vicar of Mortlake. Barnes, Mortlake and East Sheen were thereafter part of the London Borough of Richmond upon Thames.

BOOKS FOR EVERYONE

Another example of tardiness in implementing permissive legislation was the very late establishment of a public library. The 1850 Public Libraries Act was ignored until Barnes Borough Council adopted it in 1935, the last London borough to do so. But even then no provision was made, and to make good the omission Surrey County Council loaned books to students and Hammersmith and Richmond libraries allowed Barnes residents to become paying subscribers.

In 1941, when it was almost impossible to obtain books, staff or buildings, the wartime blackout led to an unprecedented demand for books and it was this that forced the borough's hand. In 1942 a small library was started in Rocks Lane, Barnes. When the war ended a former decontamination centre, roomy but damp, became available in Cleveland Road and this became the library and administrative headquarters. In 1951 the administration transferred to a prefabricated building on the site of the present Sheen Library.

The library at the Sheen Lane Centre dates from after the borough's absorption into Richmond upon Thames. The transfer of the Barnes branch library from Cleveland Road to its new site in Castelnau, planned by the old borough, also took place after the amalgamation.

84. *The official opening of the East Sheen branch library (the pre-fabricated building since replaced by the Sheen Lane Centre).
The ceremony was performed by the Mayor of Barnes, Cllr. V.R. Chadwick on 10 October 1951.*

85. *The official opening of the Castelnau branch library on 22 July 1966, by the Mayor of Richmond upon Thames, Alderman
H.A. Leon. This building replaced the library in Cleveland Road, Barnes.*

Working Lives

Before cheap workmen's rail tickets were introduced in 1883, most people worked in the area. Mortlake Brewery was the main employer, but census returns from 1871 reveal a growing number of local occupations for the unskilled and semi-skilled. For women there was domestic service in the large houses and work in at least four local laundries. Casual work for the unskilled could still be found in the market gardens: as late as 1920, Barker's of East Sheen employed 140 women to harvest, scrub and pack radishes in just one of their fields, but by 1927 the last few gardeners had left the area. Census returns for 1881-91 record a growing number of builders' labourers and artisans such as plumbers, carpenters and others employed in the construction industry, hardly surprising in view of the amount of building going on. Others worked on the railway and at the gas and waterworks.

Several small industries were started in the late nineteenth and early twentieth century. With so many wealthy residents, coach-building was introduced into East Sheen, but in time many coachhouses and stables were in use as garages for cars.

The motor car had an early impact on the area. In 1897 the newly-formed Motor Car Club held the first of several rallies at Sheen House, and in 1898 it attracted eighty vehicles. Several businesses served the early motorist: Morland's Motors in Sheen Lane was founded in 1916, and Samuel Hogger, wheelwright of Priests Bridge, turned to motor repairs: older residents still refer to the site of his business as Hogger's Corner. From 1922, cars filled-up at Cory Brothers' petrol station, on the corner of Stanley Road, East Sheen, and now a Texaco filling-station. In Barnes, Boon & Porter's Motor Garage in Castelnau and the Barnes Motor Garage in Lonsdale Road were early established. Mears Motors, an impressive garage and showroom in the Upper Richmond Road, was on the site of the present day Safeway Supermarket.

The number of sports manufacturers in the area reflect the number of clubs operating in the 1920s. From 1925 all kinds of sports equipment was manufactured in Fitzgerald Avenue, Mortlake by John Wisden, who was associated with the famous *Wisden's Cricketers' Almanack*. Not surprisingly, the firm specialised in cricket bats. Tennis rackets were manufactured by Frank Mousley in Derby Road, East Sheen: his factory, on the site of Deanhill Court, also produced matches and powder puffs!

86. The influx of wealthy residents encouraged the opening of local laundries, providing much-needed work for women. The picture shows the Lily Laundry in the former Westfields House, Charles Street, Barnes, c.1910.

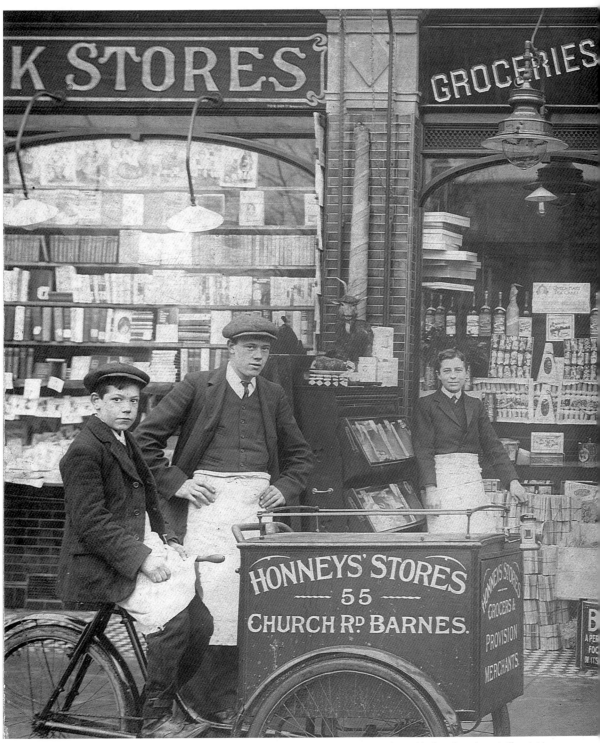

87. *Home delivery was one of the ways of keeping custom. Here, delivery boys pose, together with the other shop staff, outside Honneys' Stores at 55 Church Road, c.1920.*

88. *The Omes factory by Beverley Brook in 1962, at the end of Willow Avenue, Barnes. The firm played an important role in wartime manufacture (see p135).*

In Barnes, the lack of industry after the demise of Cowan's soap and candle factory (see p48) was partly solved by the opening of a saw-mill in Willow Avenue in 1904 by James Betts. This became the Beverley Aeroplane Works where wooden spars and other aircraft components were made during the First World War. The site was shared with a Belgian company, Lenaerts & Dolphins, who made starter motors for aircraft engines, and after the war diversified into motor car components. In 1924 they designed a limousine, the Beverley Barnes, intended to rival the Rolls Royce, but only fourteen were ever produced. The site was then acquired by Omes Works; this company were licensees of a unique electro-forging technique which played a vital part in the manufacture of components for aircraft, vehicles and armaments during World War II. The works closed in 1971 but its fine gates are preserved on the former site.

Cleveland House, a gracious eighteenth-century house on the Green, served as the Barnes and District Steam Laundry 1903-20, after which it became a small chocolate factory. In 1926 Zeeta's demolished the house and erected an extremely ugly building for a larger chocolate, ice-cream and cake factory and the smell of chocolate wafted across Barnes Green for 25 years. In 1958 the building became the Postal Sorting Office for Barnes, and it is now to be converted to residential use.

In the 1920s a landmark was the tall wireless mast on the roof of the Marconi International Marine Communications Company's premises in Barnes High Street. In Lonsdale Road, Donald McGill was trading as 'The Postcard Place' at de Vere House.

Today, with the notable exception of the Stag Brewery, hardly anyone is producing anything in any quantity in Barnes, Mortlake or East Sheen. Local workers are mostly employed in offices or in the service industries. In the 1991 census the unemployment figure was below the national average, although it contained a worrying proportion of 16-19 year-olds. Of those working in manufacturing, the highest number were in Mortlake (11% of the population), the lowest in East Sheen (5.7%). The majority of people in employment work in banking, distribution and service industries, and more than half of these are employers, managers and professionals. Most work outside the area, mainly in London.

89. A tug with a single barge in tow passing under Barnes Bridge in November 1977, the last occasion on which this commercial traffic was seen at Barnes. Joseph Locke's slender cast-iron bridge was reconstructed with wrought-iron bow girders in 1895.

On the Move

THE THAMES

Commercial traffic on the Thames, once the main means of transport, was in decline by the 1850s, though the two main wharves in Mortlake were still in use until the present century, as to a lesser extent was Small Profit Dock at Barnes. The Brewery Wharf was used occasionally until about 1960, by which time very little commercial traffic was seen on the river. In the 1950s tugs with strings of up to six barges were regularly seen passing Barnes Bridge, but one seen passing downstream in November 1977 may well have been the last. It had but a single barge in tow.

The local use of the river for leisure also declined. From the early nineteenth century pleasure steamers were a feature and in the 1840s paddle steamers for Margate picked up passengers from a wooden jetty at the White Hart, Barnes. This was short-lived, unlike the pier attached to Hammersmith Bridge from 1843 to 1921. Since then, pleasure boats seen on the river at Barnes and Mortlake are merely passing through.

90. Hammersmith Bridge 1906, with a paddle steamer about to call at the pier. Steamers called there until the First World War, but the stop was not reinstated after the war and the pier was removed in 1921.

91. The White Hart, Barnes, in 1904. A popular haunt for the rowing and sculling fraternity, and from 1840 until the First World War paddle steamers called at the pier.

ON ROADS

The two High Streets of Barnes and Mortlake were on the old road connecting the ferry at Putney, the Archbishop's manor house at Mortlake and the royal palace at Richmond. Much of this route became the Lower Richmond Road. An alternative to this, on higher and drier ground, was the Upper Richmond Road. The main route south seems to have been the road to Kingston, of which the present Sheen Lane formed part and which ran through Richmond Park, close to Ladderstile Gate. It was cut when the park was enclosed, but its course can still be partly discerned on the ground.

No trace of a direct route linking Mortlake with Wimbledon, neither trackway nor road, has ever been found, which is strange considering that Wimbledon became the centre of the former Manor of Mortlake from the late medieval period. It would seem, indeed, that it was Richmond not Wimbledon that had the greatest influence on everyday life in medieval Mortlake and over the centuries a network of lanes and tracks linked the early roads between these two places.

Motor traffic since the First World War has made the Upper Richmond Road a main through-route in and out of London and much of it became part of the orbital South Circular Road.

Compared with Mortlake, Barnes was a quiet backwater until the early nineteenth century. The High Street and the Terrace did, it is true, form part of the Lower Road to Mortlake and Richmond, and from the eighteenth century stage coaches used it. In 1798 a coach called regularly at the White Hart *en route* to London, but through travellers from London were more likely to bypass Barnes altogether, taking the more direct route along the Upper Richmond Road.

The seclusion of Barnes was broken by the opening of Hammersmith Bridge on 6 October, 1827. This first, and very narrow, suspension bridge across the Thames, designed by William Tierney Clarke and called "the wonder of the age" was, unfortunately, soon incapable of handling the traffic that wanted to use it. Sixty years later it was replaced by the present bridge, designed by Sir Joseph Bazalgette. This remains one of that engineer's finest achievements and a splendid product of the Victorian age, but in recent years the weight of traffic has rendered it unsafe. In February 1997 it was closed indefinitely to all but pedestrians, cyclists and bus passengers, and its future remains uncertain.

The bridge encouraged the development of horse bus services of which, it is said, 98 left Richmond for London daily in the 1840s. From these evolved the modern bus routes of which the No. 9 has had a particular local connection, running from 1909 to 1992 from the garage in Avondale Road, Mortlake

92. 'The Reminder' of Harwich tied up at the landing stage by Mortlake Brewery in 1939. This was the last sailing barge noted at Mortlake in commercial use.

93. *Hammersmith Bridge 1827. William Tierney Clarke was the architect and although much admired at the time, the bridge soon proved inadequate for increasing traffic. It was replaced by the present bridge in 1887.*
Engraved by George Cooke after P.D. Harding.

94. *The second Hammersmith Bridge from the roof of Castelnau Mansions. Built in 1887 to the designs of Sir Joseph Bazalgette. The complete absence of traffic except for a bus and the 'blackout' markings on the lamp posts and post box suggest a date early in the Second World War.*

95. *The first Hammersmith Bridge under construction July 1827. The lithograph is by Charles King (1773-1856), drawing master and Vestry Clerk, who lived at Suthrey House, Mortlake High Street.*

96. A No. 9 bus leaving Mortlake Bus Garage in 1983. The garage originated as stables for horse buses in 1901, and was closed and demolished in 1983.

to Liverpool Street. In recent years the route has been broken up into several sections, and in March 1997 that between Avondale Road and Hammersmith was renumbered 209. The garage, which opened as horse stables in 1901, closed in 1983.

Barnes and Mortlake never did have trams. Sir Edwin Chadwick's one intrusion into local government while living in East Sheen was in 1873, when he wrote to the Mortlake District Highway Board suggesting the use of a pair of horse-drawn trams in the parish. Having received a negative reply, Chadwick suggested trying out his scheme in Barnes, but a lukewarm answer to the effect that if the experiment failed, Chadwick was to be responsible for removing the tramway and making good the damage, seems to have ended the correspondence. From then on nothing further was ever heard of trams in either parish.

97. *A horse bus and a carriage at Hammersmith Bridge in 1906. This was the year the first motor buses appeared in Mortlake.*

98. *One of the first motor cars to cross Hammersmith Bridge, in 1906.*

99. A mishap in the Upper Richmond Road near Milestone Green, c.1914. A heavily laden steam waggon belonging to the Associated Portland Cement Manufacturers has broken its rear axle.

THE RAILWAY

A railway to run through Barnes and Mortlake was projected in 1836, but it came to nothing. It was revived as the Richmond Railway in 1845 and opened between Falcon Bridge (now Clapham Junction) and Richmond in July 1846. From the start it was supported by the London and South Western Railway (LSWR) which worked the services from its terminus at Nine Elms. Within a few months the LSWR absorbed the local company. The reason for its interest soon became clear – the route was a step to Windsor, and in 1848 the company extended the line from Richmond to Datchet and on to Windsor the following year, while at the same time the Hounslow loop line was built from Barnes, rejoining the Windsor line proper near Feltham. From the first, passenger traffic on the Windsor Lines, as the local railways have always been known, exceeded even the most optimistic of expectations, and today the railway is still one of the busiest sections in the national network. By 1885 it was necessary to quadruple the track between Clapham Junction and Barnes and in 1915-16 the local services were among the very earliest to be electrified.

Barnes Bridge on the Hounslow Loop is one of the few engineering features on the railway. Dating from the opening of the line in 1849, it was rebuilt in 1895 when the original slender three-span cast iron bridge designed by Joseph Locke was replaced by more substantial wrought-iron bow girders. Part of the original bridge survives on the up-stream side.

The Loop line has always had great importance for goods traffic through connections with the northern lines at Kew, which makes it a very useful route for traffic from the north to the south-east, a usefulness likely to grow with the opening of the Channel Tunnel.

Barnes and Mortlake were original stations on the Richmond Railway. Mortlake is still on its original site but has been rebuilt twice, the present undistinguished building dating from 1895. The original Barnes station house survives, but sadly is no longer used for railway purposes. It is notable architecturally, but the tendency of modern writers to ascribe it to Sir William Tite is not borne out by the original documents, which are silent as to the architect. The other two stations in the area were both opened later, Barnes Bridge in 1916 – the last new station to be built by LSWR – and North Sheen in 1930.

100. *The earliest picture of Barnes Station on Barnes Common, in 1857. Note the tree-less approach and the bridge carrying the Hammersmith Bridge Company's road over the railway. The banners on tall posts are early railway signals. Wash drawing by an unknown artist.*

101. *Barnes Station 1988.*

102. *Barnes Railway Bridge as built in 1849 by Joseph Locke. Elm Bank House is seen on the right. Lithograph by Charles King of Mortlake.*

103. *Barnes Station and goods yard 1954.*

104. *The railway through Mortlake, looking west from Avondale Road bridge. The railway followed the course of the Worple Way, an ancient trackway across the fields. South Worple Way to the left is the original trackway, North Worple Way to the right was laid out by the railway company. The pronounced curve approaching the station in the distance was occasioned to avoid the grounds of Portobello House.*

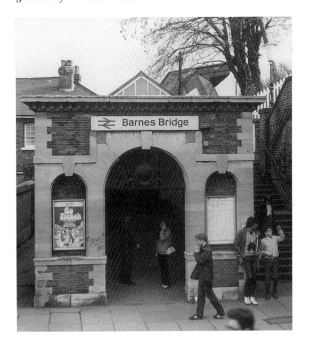

105. *(Left) Barnes Bridge station, opened in 1916, the last station to be opened by the London & South Western Railway before the grouping of railways in 1923.*

106. *(Above) A Windsor train passing Barnes in 1906.*

107. St Mary's church, Barnes, 1837, showing the early medieval nave and chapel with the tower added c.1485. The church remained thus for nearly 300 years and this view from the south never changed since subsequent additions were on the north side of the building. Lithograph by Laura Jones.

Churches and Chapels

THE PARISH CHURCHES

In medieval times there were parish churches in both Barnes and Mortlake, each dedicated to St Mary. When population increased in the nineteenth century so new Anglican churches were built, but only those in Barnes have become separate parishes.

St Mary's, Barnes has stood on its present site since the first half of the twelfth century, when it began as a small rectangular flint chapel built on a gravel mound. In a St Paul's Cathedral survey dated 1181, an unnamed priest of St Mary's is mentioned, and in 1199 Richard of Northampton was appointed there. The first enlargement of the building was probably in 1215 when, according to local tradition, the church was re-dedicated by Archbishop Stephen Langton; a tower was added *c.*1485 and more additions and extensions occurred over the centuries until 1906, when a new north aisle made it possible to seat 950. However, a disastrous fire on 8 June, 1978 brought it close to destruction – thankfully, the south and

108. Firemen fighting the fire which gutted St Mary's church on 8 June, 1978.

109. *The ruined south aisle of St Mary's, Barnes, in 1983 as restoration work began. This is the oldest part of the church, dating from c.1150.*

110. *St Mary's church, Barnes, as rebuilt in 1984. The medieval south aisle survives, restored as the Langton Chapel, as does the fifteenth-century tower.*

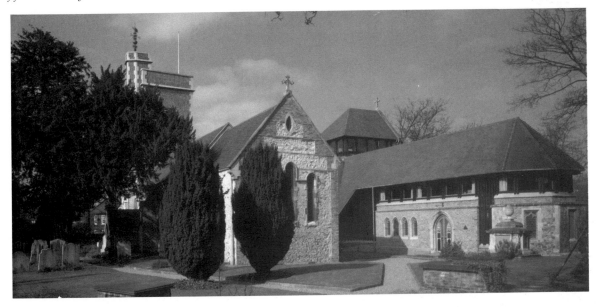

111. Strawberry House, formerly Barnes Rectory. The present house is largely as rebuilt by Francis Hare, rector 1717-27. It ceased to be a rectory in 1939 and is now a private house.

112. North view of St Mary's parish church and Mortlake High Street c.1750. The house on the right is the limner's house occupied by Francis Cleyn of the Tapestry Works. The inn sign across the street is that of the Queen's Head. Engraving by J. Roberts after J.P. Chatelain.

east walls of the medieval chapel and the Tudor tower survived. An archaeological survey after the fire dated the earliest part of the surviving building *c*.1100-1150.

From the ashes has arisen a new St Mary's, incorporating the Norman and Early English work as the Langton chapel and the main sanctuary and nave, facing north-south, with meeting rooms and church offices on either side. The architect, Edward Cullinan, has since received a number of awards for the design. The rebuilt church was rehallowed on 26 February, 1984, and today it is supported by an enthusiastic congregation which delights in the many and varied opportunities for music and drama within the main place of worship. Adjoining the church is the former Barnes Rectory, built *c*.1718, now Strawberry House.

St Mary's Mortlake is not on its original site. In medieval times it was near the manor house but on the orders of Henry VIII, possibly because it impeded alterations, it was demolished and in 1543 rebuilt on its present site. A commemorative stone in the west front of the tower marks the event:

VIVAT
RH8
1543

Nothing remains of the 1543 building apart from the tower, constructed from material salvaged from

113. John Dee (1527-1608). The most celebrated resident of Mortlake. Modern research is restoring his standing as one of the foremost Renaissance scholars.

114. Chancel of Mortlake church prior to the rebuilding of 1840. Engraved by J.M. Bayne from a drawing by Elizabeth Acworth Prinsep.

the earlier church. Its pretty cupola is an unmistakable landmark which has often proved useful in identifying old prints of Mortlake. The Vestry House dates from 1670. The fifteenth-century font presented to the medieval church by Archbishop Bourchier (1405-86) is the oldest relic, and three ancient chests, the largest of which is a superb example of medieval woodwork of German origin, are thought to have come into the church's possession in the seventeenth century. Over the years the church has been greatly altered and enlarged. Since the final extensive alterations were made in 1906 to the designs of Sir Arthur Blomfield, the structure has remained basically the same. The most recent modernisation was in 1979-1980, when a movable nave altar was installed to face a variety of positions, and the Vestry House restored.

Buried in an unmarked spot beneath the chancel are the bones of Dr John Dee (1527-1608), perhaps the most famous past resident of Mortlake. Once regarded as a wizard or necromancer, modern research has restored his standing as one of the foremost scholars of the Renaissance; a scientist, geographer and mathematician who has had few equals. His library of 4,000 books was at the time larger than that of any university. Dee was astrologer to Elizabeth I. He came to Mortlake in 1566 and lived in a house opposite the church, where he was visited by the Queen on at least two occasions.

115. St Mary's, Mortlake and the entrance to Church Path c.1900, showing the tower and much of the church being engulfed by ivy.

A GROWING POPULATION

New church building inevitably followed the suburbanisation of the area.

A chapel-of-ease to serve the new community in North Barnes was established on the west side of Castelnau in 1851 by the local developer, Major Boileau, and served by clergy from the parish church, St Mary's. But this was purely a temporary measure and by 1868 Holy Trinity Church had been built on the east side of Castelnau with seating for 289. This became a separate parish in 1880, though the Rector of Barnes retained the right to nominate the Vicar.

Additions since have included a vicarage in 1890, an enlarged chancel and vestry in 1913, and a parish room in 1954, commemorating the dead of the Second World War.

St Michael and All Angels in Elm Bank Gardens, Barnes, began as a 'school church' in 1877. A new building was consecrated in 1893 and in 1919 St Michael's became a separate parish, known for the high-church nature of its rituals.

117. Holy Trinity, Castelnau, Barnes, built in 1868. The architect, Thomas Allom, lived in Lonsdale Road.

116. Christ Church, East Sheen, 1893. It was the first church of the architect Sir Arthur Blomfield. Shortly before it was due to be finished, the newly constructed tower collapsed through faulty workmanship. Drawing by Albert Betts.

118. *The Duchess of York (now Queen Elizabeth, the Queen Mother) laying the foundation stone of All Saints', East Sheen on 24 October 1928. She revisited the church for its jubilee in 1979.*

119. *The choir and sanctuary of All Saints', East Sheen, 1932. Drawing by J.A. Noyes.*

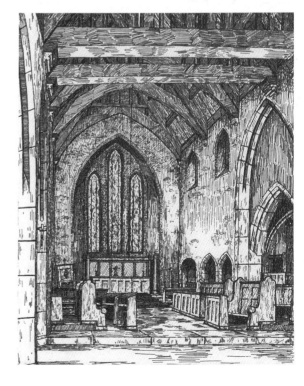

In East Sheen, Queen Victoria made the initial donation towards the building of Christ Church, designed by Sir Arthur Blomfield and consecrated in January 1864. Much later it was joined in East Sheen by All Saints. The original plan had been to build All Saints' in Clifford Avenue, but there was a change when the site in East Sheen Avenue became available. The foundation stone was laid in October 1928 by the Duchess of York, now Queen Elizabeth, the Queen Mother, and consecration was on All Saints' Day 1929. The church was rendered unusable by a serious fire in November 1965, but reopened in 1967

It was intended to build another church on the Clifford Avenue site. Here there had been an old army hut, placed there in 1921 and dedicated to St Andrew. Though a church was never built, a small but faithful congregation used the temporary building until January 1975. St Andrew's House, flats erected by the Richmond Housing Trust, are now on the site.

NONCONFORMISTS

The Mortlake Independent (later Congregational) Chapel first opened in Sheen Lane in 1716 and was closely associated with the Dutch Lutheran weavers from the Tapestry Works. It was not in continuous use but it was restored in 1836 and used until 1902, when a new church was opened by Mrs Doulton of the Lambeth Pottery firm. In October 1972 the Congregational churches joined with the Presbyterians to become the United Reformed Church.

A Baptist church, known as the Iron Church, opened in Stanton Road, Barnes, in 1866, with a seating capacity of 300. In 1934 the present church was built on the site of the former Walnut Tree Farm, a location chosen to provide a nonconformist church for North Barnes and the Castelnau Estate.

The Baptists of East Sheen worshipped for many years at the Duke Street church in Richmond, but in 1924 temporary premises were opened in Upper Richmond Road, and the church on the present site in Temple Sheen Road was opened in 1933.

Methodists first came to Barnes *c.*1860 as missionaries to a gipsy encampment on the Common. Open air meetings on Barnes Green followed and by 1867 there were sufficient followers to warrant a small chapel in White Hart Lane, and then the present church in Station Road was built in 1906 at a cost of £6,000.

This is the only Methodist church in the area, and its congregation is widely drawn. Often known as 'the Church on the Common', it has contributed much to local spiritual and social life. The old chapel in White Hart Lane is now known as the Barnes Church and Healing Centre.

120. The Dissenters' Chapel in Sheen Lane, built in 1716. The congregation, forced to leave in 1755, regained it in 1836, but the chapel was closed in 1901. It was replaced by a new church in Vernon Road. The old building was converted into shops and offices, then demolished in 1992.

Drawn by Albert Betts. 1992

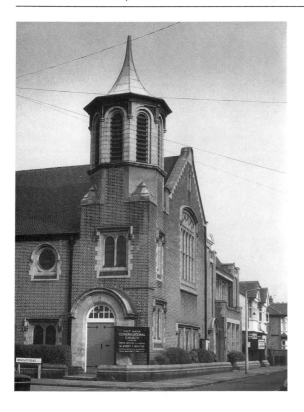

ROMAN CATHOLICS

The small Roman Catholic congregation which worshipped in a converted hayloft at Portobello House, Mortlake, was greatly increased by the arrival of Irish workers in the market gardens in the 1840s. In May 1852 a new Catholic church, St Mary Magdalen, North Worple Way, was consecrated, the cost largely met by Father Wenham the first parish priest, who lived at Acacia House, Mortlake High Street, where he also ran a boys' private school.

The Roman Catholics of Barnes had no purpose-built church until 1954. At the end of the nineteenth century they met for Mass, under the ministration of a Mortlake priest, in a small chapel attached to a girls' school in Church Road run by a community of French nuns.

In 1908 the growing congregation bought 77 Castelnau, where a large room in the house was adapted for worship, and the rest housed the congregation's own priest. By 1928 sufficient money was raised to build a temporary church on an adjoining garden plot, and eventually no. 79 was also taken to serve as the priest's house. The buildings on the earlier site were subsequently demolished and St Osmund's Church was opened in 1954, much delayed by the war.

121. (Top left) East Sheen Congregational Church (now the United Reformed Church) and Vernon Hall, Vernon Road, 1969. It was built in 1902, replacing the chapel in Sheen Lane.

122. (Top right) Barnes Methodist church in Station Road, soon after it was built in 1906.

123. (Below) St Osmund's Roman Catholic church in Castelnau, built in 1950.

The Dear Departed

THE PARISH CHURCHYARDS

Until the middle of the nineteenth century people were buried in the parish churchyards. At St Mary's, Barnes, post-fire excavations identified the site of the earliest burial ground to the west of the twelfth-century chapel. Tombstones in this well-kept churchyard reflect a cross-section of parish life long gone. The bones of market gardeners and watermen, innkeepers and millers, school-masters and doctors lie alongside those of Captain Dawson (1795-1859), claimed by his family to be the son of Mrs Fitzherbert and the Prince Regent, and Sir Lancelot Shadwell (1779-1850), last Vice-Chancellor of England, and father to seventeen children by his two wives. He is said to have bathed daily in the lake at Barn Elms where he lived from 1835 until his death. One of his many sons drowned in the lake.

There is a war memorial to parishioners who died in two world wars, and another by the lych gate for the fallen in the Boer War. The churchyard was closed for further burials in 1854.

The churchyard of St Mary's, Mortlake is still bounded by the wall of John Dee's garden (see p88). The ground was granted to the parish by Henry VIII in 1543, when the church was rebuilt on its new site, and extended in 1742 and 1799. Buried there among the ordinary folk of Mortlake are a Prime Minister (Lord Sidmouth) and three eighteenth-century Lord Mayors of London. The earliest surviving tomb is of John Partridge, astrologer and almanack maker (d.1715).

The churchyard was closed for burials in 1854 and a new cemetery opened in South Worple Way. In recent years a fund was launched to restore the overgrown churchyard along with many of its ancient tombstones. It is now a quiet green refuge from the busy traffic in Mortlake High Street and is carefully tended by the Friends of Mortlake Churchyard.

124. The Lancaster Memorial (1920) in East Sheen cemetery, one of the most notable examples of modern monumental sculpture. The artist is not known.

125.   *The entrance to the cemetery on Barnes Common c.1910, showing the keeper's lodge and chapel.*

NEW CEMETERIES

Both Barnes and Mortlake opened cemeteries when the parish churchyards were closed in 1854. That for Barnes was laid out on two acres enclosed from Barnes Common. Among several distinguished Victorians buried in what was later called Barnes Old Cemetery is Sir Francis Palgrave (1824-1897), compiler of the *Golden Treasury of English Verse*. This cemetery was closed in 1954 and the railings removed, so that this once-neat burial ground is now dreadfully vandalised, and a thick carpet of brambles covers the broken tombstones. Management is in the hands of the local authority, which has designated the area a nature reserve.

Mortlake Old Cemetery is on land near Barnes Hospital and in 1874 was extended across old market garden land. Burials here include those of John Eustace Anderson, vestry clerk and local historian, Sir Edwin Chadwick and two relatives of the novelist Charles Dickens – his son Charles, and his sister-in-law and housekeeper, Georgina Hogarth.

Most local burials are now at East Sheen Cemetery, which was opened in 1903. This is notable for a magnificent *Art Nouveau* bronze monument, known as the Angel of Death, which commemorates George Lancaster, *c.*1920 and his wife Louisa, who lived at Clare Lawn, East Sheen.

126.   *The chapel in Mortlake cemetery, South Worple Way. It was never consecrated, and was demolished in 1969.*

SMALLER GRAVEYARDS

The churchyard of St Mary Magdalen's Roman Catholic church in North Worple Way, contains the tomb of Sir Richard Burton (1821-90), author, diplomat, explorer and translator of *The Arabian Nights* and *The Perfumed Garden*, and his wife Isobel. The stone tomb, in the form of an Arab tent, contains a small altar and two gilt coffins set with coloured glass. Lady Isobel lived at 65 North Worple Way from 1891 and made daily visits to her husband's tomb, sometimes sitting inside. As the massive stone door was opened, strings of camel bells would tinkle. Each year on 22 January, a Mass of repose is said for the Burtons' souls.

A tiny burial ground for the use of dissenters who preferred not to take up the option of an unconsecrated area in their own parish churchyard, was opened in 1842 in Mortlake. It is now an overgrown and rubbish-strewn ground, but the threat of building development on it has recently been lifted.

127. (Below) The tomb of Sir Richard Burton in the churchyard of the Roman Catholic church of St Mary Magdalen. It is in the shape of an Arab tent.

128. (Right) The Dissenters' graveyard behind the former British School in South Worple Way in 1965, seen from Princes Road.

Local Inns

An alehouse in Barnes, known as the Rose, appears in records of 1632. In 1690 it became a dwelling house, part of which survives as Rose House, 70 Barnes High Street, the home of the Barnes Community Association since 1974. In 1649 the 'Sign of the Rayne Deer' stood facing the river near the end of Barnes High Street, the landlord Thomas Reeve. For a while it was the King's Head and by 1735 it was rebuilt as the Bull's Head, which still stands on the site. Since 1952 it has become a widely known venue for the best in modern jazz.

Further to the west facing the river, on the boundary with Mortlake, was the King's Arms in 1662; at some time in the eighteenth century it became the White Hart. Rebuilt several times, the present large house dates from 1899. Always popular with rowers, the White Hart's commanding position on the riverside just above Barnes Bridge has for many years been a favourite viewing point for the Oxford and Cambridge Boat Race. In the 1920s, spectators filled 200 reserved seats on its balconies, plus several unreserved standing places.

Another well-known Barnes pub is the Red Lion, near the junction of Castelnau and Rocks Lane – it is recorded in 1718, when a James Singer was admitted to the property which in those days would have had nothing but farmland to the north. After a fire in 1835, it was rebuilt as the present Red Lion. Two popular Barnes pubs, dating from the eighteenth century are the Coach & Horses in the High Street, with a garden at the rear, and the Sun Inn facing Barnes Pond, which may date back a little further.

The Ship on Thames Bank, is thought to be the oldest existing Mortlake inn. Much changed over the centuries, it stands by the river on roughly the same

129. The interior of the Old George, as drawn by Albert Betts in 1893.

130. Clipson's beerhouse was built for the Hammersmith Bridge Company, which enclosed part of Barnes Common at the junction of Rocks Lane and the Upper Richmond Road. Later rebuilt as the Railway Hotel, the house was renamed the Red Rover after the last war, from the stage coach which once ran from London to Southampton. It was closed as a public house in 1989 and after some years as a cafe/wine bar now awaits demolition.

131. *Of the many inns in Mortlake, the Old George was one of the oldest, the first record being 1700. Shown here c.1914, the building was probably early nineteenth century, but is of interest in being end-on to the High Street, a relic of the old medieval strips. It closed in 1968, replaced by the Charlie Butler, and now lies under the widened High Street.*

132. *The Red Lion in Edwardian days. It dates back to at least the eighteenth century, and was at one time called the Strugglers.*

133. *The Queen's Head, c.1875, which was built in the early eighteenth century. Access was by the narrow alley from Mortlake High Street. It was rebuilt in the 1890s and closed in 1932, but it survives as flats known as Tapestry Court. The ruined building on the left is the Lower Dutch House of the Tapestry Works, which was restored as flats in 1877 and demolished in 1950 after wartime damage. Lithograph by Albert Betts.*

134. *The Plough in Christ Church Road, East Sheen, before 1914, with Merton Cottages beyond. The latter date back to the 17th-18th centuries and during recent alterations traces of a fifteenth-century wall were uncovered in the Plough.*

135.   *The Boileau in Castelnau, near Hammersmith Bridge. Built in 1842 with the first villas in the road, it was known then as the Boileau Arms. It remains open and has changed little, except that it is now the Garden House restaurant.*

site it has occupied since the sixteenth century, when it was the Harteshorn, and later the Blew Anchor. Standing as it did close to an ancient landing place, its early customers would have mostly been watermen and their passengers.

Other eighteenth-century Mortlake inns were the King's Head, the Old George, the Three Tuns and the Queen's Head. The King's Head had regular standings for twelve horses and was the only hostelry offering horses and chaises for hire. Incorporated into the brewery in the nineteenth century, it survived as the Mortlake Hotel until 1955. The Old George, an alehouse dating from *c*.1700 went with the widening of Mortlake High Street in 1968 and was replaced by the Charlie Butler. The Three Tuns dating from 1740, was later the Jolly Gardeners; the present house of that name dates from 1922. The Queen's Head, featured in many depictions of the Mortlake riverside, was converted into flats in 1952.

In East Sheen there were two large inns on the north side of the Upper Richmond Road. The Hare & Hounds still stands on its original site to the east of the Sheen Lane crossroads, but the more important of the two was the Bull at Sheen. Its date of origin is uncertain, more likely seventeenth than eighteenth century. It

stood west of the crossroads and had stabling, yard and outbuildings reaching back into Sheen Lane. Sadly, nothing remains of this once renowned coaching inn, not even its name. The old Bull was demolished in 1937, and the new Bull, built in the same year, was pulled down in 1987. Further south along Sheen Lane, Thomas Strutt owned the Plough at East Sheen in 1733, occupying what had been three old cottages. During recent structural work, fifteenth-century timber framing was uncovered.

New pubs were built in the nineteenth-century developments. The Victoria appeared in East Sheen, where its profusion of hanging baskets and boxes filled with colourful plants is one of the regular delights of summer. The Derby Arms, dating from the last quarter of the century, when it was popular with market gardeners, has recently been converted to flats. In Barnes, the development of Castelnau brought the Bridge Hotel and the Boileau Arms, known to many bus conductors as 'the Boiler'. The latter lost its local connections by being twice renamed and is presently a pub/restaurant, the Garden House. The present owners agreed to retain the Boileau family's coat-of-arms on the front exterior, at the request of local residents.

136. The Wheatsheaf and Hampton Square, off Sheen Lane, 1904. The pub was demolished after the last war and the Sheen Lane Centre now occupies the site. Drawing by W. Lewis Turner.

Other newcomers in the nineteenth century served the two working-class areas of Barnes and Mortlake. These were modest beerhouses, built when the temperance movement was gaining ground. Upper and middle-class voices were raised against the licensees and their encouragement of drunken behaviour among the labouring classes, forgetful of the fact that the pub was often the only form of social life available to them, and sometimes the only means of escape from a wretched environment. In the 1830s, visiting Poor Law Commissioners reported that the local labour force was not so industrious as before, owing to the many drinking houses. Particularly notorious was the Wheatsheaf in Sheen Lane. Reports of its Saturday night fights and the regular drunken brawling of its patrons – market garden labourers for the most part from nearby Hampton Square – used up a great deal of ink in the local press. In 1875 the *Richmond and Twickenham Times* featured the Wheatsheaf as one of the "sinks and dens" of its circulation area.

Well-intentioned alternatives to the demon drink were the Welcome Coffee Palace and Mission Hall in the Westfields, Barnes and the Mission Hall in Mortlake High Street. Judging by the number of beerhouses which survived these were not entirely successful. The Wheatsheaf lived on until 1962; the Halfway House, the Market Gardener, Rose of Denmark, Edinburgh Castle and the Manor Arms remain in the Westfields/Priests Bridge area of Barnes. Mortlake has the Railway Tavern in Sheen Lane and the Queen's Arms in Princes Road. Their nineteenth-century patrons would, however, find it difficult to identify with the smart appearance of the former beerhouses today.

Recent decisions to rename the Jolly Milkman and the Market Gardener have now been reversed. In the present century just two new public houses have been built. One is the Charlie Butler, opened in 1968 to replace the Old George, when Mortlake High Street was widened. The other, built in 1987 facing Sheen Lane, occupies a small corner of the site of the lost Bull. Most local people expected it be named the Bull, but the owners decided on the Pig and Whistle.

137. *The Railway Tavern, Sheen Lane, viewed from Mortlake Green, c.1930. The house dates back to c.1800 and is one of the oldest surviving houses in Mortlake. It was converted into a tavern in 1846 when the railway opened. The adjacent shops have gone, those to the right converted into flats but retaining the unusual facade.*

138. *The Edinburgh Castle in White Hart Lane, Barnes. A Victorian pub which still survives, but sadly the ornamental ironwork around the roof has gone.*

Places of Learning

Before the nineteenth century, any education the poorer village children received was mostly dependent on charitable bequests. For example, Joanna Hullenberch's will of 1662 specified that her bequest to Mortlake parish was for "the puttinge ffourthe of poore fatherless and motherless Children apprentices". Education in this instance consisted of being taught a trade.

During the eighteenth century other bequests supported local charity schools. In 1722 such a school was established for 22 poor children in the Vestry House, Mortlake, and in 1775 another was begun in Barnes, where two cottages belonging to Richard Hoare on the Green were let to the parish for ten boys and ten girls to be educated and clothed in a prescribed uniform. Idleness in the poor was something to be deplored and the aim of these schools was to encourage industry and temper it with docility.

Both schools were financed in a similar fashion. Firstly there were bequests, left in the case of Mortlake by Lady Dorothy Capel and Edward Colston among others, and secondly money collected at an annual charity sermon given in the parish church. Further income came from a committee of annual subscribers or trustees.

NATIONAL SCHOOLS

By 1818 both charity schools were under the management of the National Society for the Education of the Poor in the Principles of the Established Church, and therefore closely allied with the parish churches. They were expanded to include all the children who wished to attend, and not just the very poor. In Barnes, pupils over seven years paid 1d a week, those aged two to seven paid 2d. A Mr Roseblade was headmaster in 1818 and he was still in charge in 1849, when he died aged 77.

Both parishes adopted the monitorial system for teaching large classes, in which the brighter pupils

139. The National Schools, Mullins Path, assembled for Empire Day 1909. The houses in the background are in Fitzgerald Road with Scarborough Lodge on the extreme left. The cottages in the centre are Adelaide and Honeysuckle.

140. *The National Schools, Mullins Path. A class in the 1920s.*

141. The rules of the Mortlake Charity Schools in 1836.

augmented the minimal teaching staff and helped educate the other pupils – this could lead to an apprenticeship as a pupil teacher, with a gratuity on leaving the school. Subscribers' Minute Books for the Barnes school show that much of the teaching was taken up with religious education and the 'three Rs', with carpentry for the boys and needlework for the girls.

In Mortlake, between 1815 and 1819, a schoolroom was erected on part of the nearby workhouse garden; this became the Infant School in 1843 when the former workhouse was converted into a school for older boys and girls. Then in 1869, the school was enlarged, with separate departments for boys and girls. Thomas Leaney was appointed headmaster of what was then known as Mortlake Church School, a post he held for 44 years. In 1890 a new Infants' School was opened, helped by a generous contribution from one of the wealthy residents in East Sheen, the Duke of Fife.

The Barnes school was dreadfully overcrowded until 1854 when the premises were rebuilt and enlarged. Even so, eleven years later there were sixty boys in one room and 116 girls and infants being taught together in another.

Both of these schools, as the full title of the National Society suggests, were intended to extend the influence of the Church of England, but in 1843, a British School for children of nonconformists was opened in South Worple Way, Mortlake, largely due to the efforts of Dr Gosling Townley, minister to the Congregational church. It taught quite a wide range of subjects to its boy pupils, but girls were less fortunate. After a chequered history it closed its doors in 1871.

Children from Roman Catholic families attended a school attached to St Mary Magdalen's, and in 1853 53 boys and girls were presented for examination. Extensions and the addition of a new infants' school in 1859 met the need for more provision.

A free Ragged School was opened in Malthouse Passage, Barnes, for "the gutter children, the poorest of the poor", financed by an endowment of £3,000 given by James Hedgman of Elm Bank House, The Terrace. Very little in the way of teaching went on there, but the children were given two free meals a day.

142. (Top) The National Schools in Mullins Path, Mortlake, c.1900. The house to the right is the former workhouse and still stands as Capel Court. Drawing by Albert Betts.

143. (Bottom) The British School in South Worple Way in 1969. Closed as a school in 1871, the building stood until 1996.

STATE INTERVENTION

Under the Elementary Education Act of 1870 District School Boards were set up all over the country and their schools gradually superseded those of the National and British Societies. The Act resulted in the opening of a second school in Barnes: the girls and infants stayed at the school on the Green, but the boys moved to a building at the junction of Archway Street and Cross Street in Westfields, which acted as a combined church and school until St Michael's opened in 1894.

Small government grants meant surprise visits from the School Inspector. In 1878 the Inspector judged conditions at the Barnes boys' school to be "deplorable". The floor was filthy, the playground was covered in smelly pools and the pupils were barely up to the mark in any subject. The Green School was even worse: "the babies are learning nothing and are in great confusion. The needlework is remarkably filthy and reading books and drinking water would be a good idea." Gradually new buildings were erected and conditions improved. A school for girls and infants opened in Westfields in 1880 and another in Fanny Road (St Hilda's Road) in North Barnes in 1883. The latter was the only one in Barnes to earn praise from the Inspector. Today none of these buildings exists apart from the Green School, now a Day Centre for the elderly.

COUNCIL SCHOOLS

In 1902 County Council schools replaced the Board schools and another building programme began. The first school in Barnes solely for infants was opened in Railway Street (Westfields Avenue) in 1904, which today does excellent work as the Westfields Primary School in greatly expanded premises. In Mortlake a school for the newly built-up area near the brewery in the Lower Richmond Road was opened on a two-acre site near the junction with Kingsway. At first the children made do with temporary buildings but in January 1905 the over-sevens moved into a two-storey brick building, with separate accommodation for girls and boys. It was four years before the infants were able to leave their temporary quarters and occupy their own single storey building. By the 1920s this had become the Junior Mixed and Infant School. The school leaving age had been raised to fourteen in 1918 and the larger of the two buildings was converted into two Central Schools, one for boys, the other for girls, the first of their kind to provide specialised education for 11-14 year-olds from the whole Mortlake area. The Central Schools soon earned an excellent reputation and the boys were particularly successful in music, handicrafts and physical education. The schools were closed in 1969.

State education came late to East Sheen, for the affluence of the area before its intensive development

144. Barnes Green School on the east side of Barnes Pond. The buildings still stand and are now used as a Day Centre for the elderly.

145. *(Top) The 'Babies' room at Mortlake Junior and Infants' School, c.1927. It was latterly Mortlake Green School.*

146. *(Bottom) Mortlake Central Schools in Lower Richmond Road, 1920s.*

rendered it hardly necessary. But in 1913 the first East Sheen Council School was opened in the Upper Richmond Road. East Sheen Primary School now occupies the site – it is one of two well-regarded state primaries in East Sheen, the other being Sheen Mount, opened in 1954.

When it was built *c.*1926, the LCC Castelnau Estate posed problems, for the 640 houses were for families only and the school age population in Barnes therefore rose sharply. After some delays, a new school for the younger children was built in Stillingfleet Road – this flourishes today as Lowther Primary. The Barnes Central School for Boys had been opened in Lonsdale Road in 1920 with a Central School for Girls built alongside later. The boys' school was extended to accommodate the older boys from the Castelnau Estate and the older girls were found places in the existing school.

There was no selective grammar school education until East Sheen County School for Boys opened in Park Avenue in 1926. Girls waited until 1931 for a similar school to be built in Hertford Avenue, but this was temporarily closed in 1939 as most of the pupils were evacuated.

Since World War II, state education has undergone many changes in Barnes and Mortlake. Following the 1944 Education Act, Mortlake Church School became voluntary aided and falling numbers led to its closure in 1982. Most of the buildings were cleared for housing but the Infant School survives as a nursery school and public hall. Many pupils transferred to the school in Lower Richmond Road, known from 1974 as Mortlake Green Primary. This too was closed in 1988. St Mary Magdalen's Roman Catholic church school is now the sole provider of primary education north of the railway line. The two Central Schools in Lonsdale Road were demolished shortly after the pupils had left in 1977 for the new comprehensive, Shene School, which occupies the old East Sheen County School in Park Avenue. Today, Shene School draws its pupils from the whole borough of Richmond upon Thames.

PRIVATE ACADEMIES

There were many private schools in the larger houses of the area from the nineteenth century onwards. Among the more important in Barnes were Mrs Elwall's School 'for the higher education of the daughters of gentlemen', and Cleveland House Academy and Nassau House School both for 'the sons of gentlemen'.

Mrs Elwall opened her school in Milbourne House in 1823. Pupils aged four to fourteen were taught a wide range of subjects with a thorough grounding for public examinations. Innumerable extra subjects were available, from elocution to wood carving. The school was highly successful and soon required bigger premises, and when a move was made across the Green to Hillersdon House, a daughter took over from Mrs Elwall and finally the care passed to Miss Eliza Beale, sister of Dorothea, first Head of Cheltenham Ladies' College. The school was open until 1895, and after it closed Hillersdon House was demolished.

Cleveland House Academy, founded in 1800, was carried on by Dr John Palin until his death in 1852, after which it continued for a few more years. The boys boarded in a large house backing on to Barnes pond and played games on the Green. Among other

147. *The Cleveland House Academy, from a school prospectus. The school occupied Cleveland House, which stood on the west side of Barnes Green until the 1920s.*

148. *The Convent School in Church Road, Barnes, opposite the Green.*

149. *Boys of the South West London College at 99-101 Castelnau, c.1919. The headmaster was Ernest Burbidge and the fourth boy from the left in the second row is believed to be Errol Flynn.*

150. A boy at Temple Grove School mid-19th century.

requirements, the pupils were requested to bring a silver spoon and fork.

Nassau House School was founded in 1859 by Professor Attwell. Judging by what is known of their subsequent careers, the pupils aged six to eighteen were extremely well taught, for many rose high in their chosen professions of medicine, science, politics and the armed forces. The school was of comparatively short duration and closed in 1881.

At the turn of the century a community of French nuns opened the Convent of the Sacred Heart High School for Young Ladies in Church Road, Barnes. Two adjoining houses were taken by the sisters and extra premises were built in the large garden for classrooms and sleeping accommodation. Boys were accepted up to the age of 7, but girls could stay until 16 plus. The standard of work was high, good manners were expected and an excellent community spirit was engendered among the pupils. The school closed in 1969 and the buildings now house St Osmund's R.C. Primary School.

A well-known school in Barnes was Beverley House

School, which began in a small way in Beverley Road *c.*1866, then transferred under the headship of Corelli Stevens to The Laurels on Barnes Green some thirty years later. This was a day and boarding school and although pupils could stay on to finish their education a number left early having gained entrance to public schools. When Stevens retired, the school continued for a while in Castelnau and then Church Road; it closed its doors during World War II.

Briefly, the South-West London College in Castelnau had the young Errol Flynn for a pupil. In his autobiography, *My Wicked, Wicked Ways*, Flynn elaborated on his days there, when the school was run by Dr and Mrs Burbidge.

In September 1968 the famous public school, St Paul's, together with its preparatory school Colet Court, moved into Barnes, where they occupy a former reservoir site in Lonsdale Road. Nearby is a Swedish School and, a little further to the west, the latest independent school to arrive in Barnes, which uses the former house and sports club belonging to Harrods and therefore calls itself the Harrodian School.

Very little is known about the private schools of Mortlake and East Sheen apart from their names. Day and Boarding Schools for girls in Mortlake, included one in 1839 run by Caroline and Susan Kishere of the Pottery family, Ashleigh College based in Castelnau House, Mortlake High Street between 1895 and 1907, and several smaller establishments.

In the years between 1905-24 there were schools in East Sheen which extended the education of girls and acted as preparatory schools for boys. One of these, East Sheen College, paid, according to its brochure, special attention to the cultivation of refined manners. Palewell Park School gave sound and practical education for girls up to sixteen, and there was Sheen Gate House, a long established school, which closed in 1974.

One school in East Sheen was quite outstanding – that begun by the Rev. William Pearson soon after he bought the former home of the Palmerston family in 1810. He named it Temple Grove and its reputation as a preparatory school for the leading public schools grew rapidly; its sale in 1817 to the Rev. John Pinckney only added to its national standing. Numbered among its many distinguished ex-pupils are George Bell, Bishop of Chichester and Tyrone Guthrie, the actor. The school moved to Eastbourne in 1907 and later to Heron's Ghyll, Sussex, where it still flourishes.

One private school survives in East Sheen, the thriving Tower House Preparatory School for boys in Sheen Lane.

Ways of Caring

THE AGED POOR

The Poor Law Act of 1601 placed the care of the poor in the hands of parishes, which were able to levy a poor rate. In 1742 the Overseers of the Poor for Barnes allowed 2/6d a week to John Stansby and his wife who "being ancient" were "in great want". The Overseers were local men elected annually at the Easter Vestry meeting, and knowing the parishioners they were able to distinguish between the 'deserving poor' and the 'malingerers'. Mary Ayres, for example, who had "an estate of £5 a year and was able to work", was refused an allowance. Elderly widows often received extra allowances for fostering orphaned babies and infants. These unfortunate 'nurse children' appeared far too often in the parish burial registers.

Before the Poor Law Act, charitable bequests of wealthier parishioners had provided food, clothing and even housing. Overseers' account books for Barnes and Mortlake mention "loaves of good, sweet and wholesome bread", and greatcoats and sacks of coal given to aged men and women who attended Sunday service at the parish church.

John Juxon's will, dated 1626, provided housing for "foure poore widows" in the parish of Mortlake. Further gifts were added to this bequest and today Juxon's Almshouses stand at the corner of Milton and Upper Richmond Roads, with sufficient accommodation for four inhabitants. In 1707, Edward Colston built cottages near Milestone Green for the benefit of the needy in Mortlake, but made no provision for their upkeep. Their successors stand on a new site at the corner of Well Lane and Christchurch Road, East Sheen, able to house up to six people, having been maintained by church rates and other donations. Both groups of almshouses have been modernised and adapted for the needs of the elderly.

Other almshouses in Mortlake, extraordinary for their elaborately ornate appearance, were built by the Boot and Shoe Makers' Benevolent Association in 1836 and known locally as 'All Soles'; the fourteen dwellings with a chapel in the centre were all front and practically no back. The almshouses were damaged in World War II and now, with many of their decorative features removed and the chapel rebuilt as a dwelling, they are the much altered, privately owned Rosemary Cottages.

Small sums left by Mrs Diana Savage in 1726 and Mr Peter Marquet in 1730 were to provide tenements for the aged poor of Barnes. By 1750, three dwellings, referred to in the vestry minutes as 'armes houses', had been purchased, probably at the river end of the High Street. These continued in use until 1827, when funds from the Hammersmith Bridge Company enabled them to be replaced by a row of three one-

151. Barnes High Street from the Pond, showing three tiny, single-storied almshouses built in the mid-19th century. They were demolished in 1937.

152. Juxon's Almshouses, Church Path, East Sheen. They were built c.1746 and demolished in 1911, when they were rebuilt with their frontages facing Milton Road.

153. Milestone Green and Colston's Almshouses, 1893. The viewpoint is north from the present war memorial with Sheen Lane opposite and the Upper Richmond Road running across the centre. The almshouses were demolished in 1922 and rebuilt on a new site in Christ Church Road. Drawing by Albert Betts.

storied, single roomed dwellings, with a shared water tap and a 'necessary' at the rear. These stood at the corner of the High Street and Station Road and were in use for the next hundred years. They were finally demolished in August 1937.

154. Another view of Colston's Almshouses and Milestone Green, in c.1914.

155. Mortlake Station c.1900 with the Boot and Shoe Makers' Almshouses to the right. The almshouses still stand but they have lost their grand frontage.

IN THE WORKHOUSE

From about 1722, parishes were encouraged to build premises where the poor of all ages could be housed and given work to pay for their keep. In 1732 Mortlake erected a workhouse behind the High Street, close to the church, and the Barnes workhouse was built in 1778 on the extreme south-eastern edge of the parish on a triangular piece of land enclosed from the Common between Queen's Ride and the Upper Richmond Road. Both parishes kept detailed accounts of their workhouses. Diet, rigid rules of behaviour, daily tasks, the education – or more properly, the lack of education – of the children, brawls among inmates and in the case of Barnes, the rape of a 9-year-old female pauper, were all recorded. Outdoor relief was still given, especially to the elderly.

The parish workhouses were fairly small: the average population of the Barnes house was around thirty, far removed from the 'New Bastilles' in other places that resulted from the Poor Law Amendment Act of 1834.

In 1836 the newly-created Richmond Board of Guardians opened the Richmond Union Workhouse, a large building in Grove Road, to which all the inhabitants of the neighbouring workhouses were transferred, including those from Barnes and Mortlake. The workhouse in Mortlake became a school (see p105) and in Barnes part of the site was leased for market gardening and the house became a private residence and later a hotel, dignified by the name,

156. The Old Pest House, East Sheen. Given to the parish in 1668, it stood near Palewell Common. It was sold to William Gilpin of Palewell Lodge in 1845 and subsequently demolished.

The Manor House. Today, blocks of flats and houses cover the entire site. The money raised by the sale of the land was invested and is managed by the Barnes Workhouse Trust whose trustees distribute funds to a wide variety of causes, strictly within the parish of Barnes.

SELF-HELP

Poverty remained a perpetual anxiety for vast numbers of people before the days of the Welfare State. Winter was a bad time for outdoor workers, when men in trades such as building might be out of work for weeks on end. In Barnes and Mortlake, local church organisations stepped in on these occasions with soup kitchens, but not all the poorer members of society were willing to resort to charity or to the workhouse. Those who were in work and could afford a few pennies a week sought to protect themselves against bad times by joining coal, blanket and clothing clubs run in both parishes by the church.

From the early nineteenth century the desire for self-help is evident in the number of Friendly Societies in Mortlake. Eight were registered between 1801 and 1867, mostly based on local public houses, but one, the Mortlake Friendly Society for Women, founded in 1802, gave its registered address as the Mortlake Vestry Room. This Society lasted until 1949.

THE SICK

There has never been a General Hospital in Barnes or Mortlake. From time to time records refer to a pest house near Palewell Common where victims of cholera or other infectious diseases were isolated. In 1832 during a particularly bad outbreak of cholera, when there were 35 victims in Mortlake, a cottage near the workhouse was fitted up as a hospital under the care of four local doctors who made up the Board of Health, but no cases were admitted. It was more usual to treat the sick in their own homes.

In 1889 a specialist hospital for the treatment of infectious diseases was opened in South Worple Way, after much local protest. Formerly known as the Isolation Hospital, it has outlived its original use and as Barnes Hospital it is used today as a day care hospital or long term home for geriatric patients. The area is served by excellent health centres, but the future of Queen Mary's University Hospital in Roehampton, the 'local hospital' for Barnes and Mortlake for many years, has recently become a subject for concern.

157. *Mortlake's only cinema, the Gaiety, in 1961. It stood in Mortlake High Street between the Old George and the Two Brewers. Built in 1913, it closed as a cinema in 1930, but survived in commercial use until gutted by fire in 1961.*

Stage and Screen

THE GAIETY

For a time, Mortlake and East Sheen each had a cinema of its own, and Barnes had a cinema which became a theatre.

A small cinema owned by the Mortlake Cinema Company at 44-46 Mortlake High Street opened on 29 December, 1913, and apart from a temporary closure during the First World War, the Gaiety gave more or less regular performances until it closed on 31 July, 1930. Used briefly as a storehouse by the Flush Block Co. of Fulham, the building then stood derelict for some years until its demolition in the road widening of the late 1960s.

The Gaiety was typical of its kind. A pay-box was housed centrally in the entrance foyer, which opened directly into the 408-seat auditorium. The cinema was conveniently situated between public houses and regular patrons were known to pop out for a quick pint during boring bits in the programme, safe in the knowledge that the manager would allow them back in for no extra charge. Others made use of the

nearby fish and chip shop before entering, and the smell from their warm newspaper parcels permeated the auditorium. Saturday afternoon audiences were mostly schoolchildren, who also enjoyed firing peashooters at the screen, or at each other, often resulting in the manager stopping the film and ejecting the offenders. For all its shortcomings, the Gaiety was enjoyed by the locals and much missed when it closed.

LUXURY AND FREE TEA IN EAST SHEEN

Altogether different from the Gaiety was the Picturedrome in East Sheen, opened on 26 December, 1910, and advertised in the local press as "the most luxurious electric theatre around London". It occupied the site of an old house, The Larches, at the junction of Upper Richmond Road and Sheen Lane. Among its attractions was free afternoon tea for matinée patrons in the 6d and 1s seats. Early in 1920 it gained publicity with an exclusive showing of *Broken Blossoms*, starring Lillian Gish, direct from the west end of London. The Picturedrome was demolished in 1929 to make way for the Sheen Kinema. The Sheen was one of three cinemas designed for

158. *The War Memorial at the Triangle, East Sheen (formerly Milestone Green), shortly after it was erected in 1925. Behind it is Sheen's first cinema, the Picturedrome, which opened in 1910 and was replaced by the Kinema in 1930.*

159. The Sheen Kinema on a winter's evening in 1938. The main film is 'Break the News' with Jack Buchanan.

160. The Sheen Kinema as the Odeon, c.1960.

Joseph Theatres Ltd by the eminent architects Leathart and Grainger, and was of the style later known as 'pre-war Odeon'. It seated 1404 in stalls and circle and boasted a Christie 2 manual organ to the left of the pit. Its exterior was designed to attract a night-time audience: on dark evenings its illuminated appearance was stunning, the lighting reflected in the white and green glazed facing of the building to great effect.

In 1940 the Sheen Kinema became the Empire and in 1944 it was the Odeon. Sadly, it closed on 3 July, 1961 and was later demolished.

A CREATIVE THEATRE

During the early years of this century Byfield House and Nithwater House in Barnes were demolished and, fronting on Church Road, Byfeld Hall and Lowther Mansions, with the shops forming Lowther Parade were built.

Byfeld Hall was completed in 1906. Designed in a mildly flamboyant Dutch baroque style, the architect was probably J. Harrison, although the name of Arthur Osborn has also been suggested. The cupola originally surmounting the rather squat tower on the south-eastern corner was removed in the early 1960s.

The main hall on the first floor, measured 53 x 43ft and had accommodation for 350 with a further 150 in the gallery; there was also a smaller hall within the complex.

The opening events of 20 December, 1906 included a bioscope show, and after that the halls were used for theatricals, dances, concerts, whist drives, meetings and children's parties. From 1910, the hall operated as the Cinematograph Theatre opening on 4 June, with a programme including views of Edward VII's funeral, during which time Miss Kathleen Mackenzie sang *Nearer my God to Thee*. For the next fifteen years the hall went under various managements and names including Barnes Cinema, New Byfeld Picture Hall and Barnes Picture House.

In 1925, a young theatrical producer, Philip Ridgeway, acquired the lease to create Barnes Theatre. He aimed to produce plays which were a cut above the fare then available in the west end and, working on a tight budget, planned to transfer some of his productions into central London. He engaged different casts for each production and was able to attract established actors for minimal salaries with the promise of innovative work. In the event the first four productions, all new plays with accomplished casts, though well enough received in Barnes, did not transfer and none has survived.

In June 1925, during the run of the third play, *Make Your Fortune*, a farcical comedy by Elizabeth Rae, there was such a heat wave and consequent loss of business that Ridgeway erected a fit-up theatre on Barnes Common, which proved very popular – but only briefly, for it was found that Ridgeway had in the process enclosed common land, and the theatre was closed after three performances. But. the popu-

161. The Byfeld Hall and adjacent shops shortly after they were built in 1906. Except for the end tower, the block survives and after a colourful career as a theatre and cinema, the Hall continues in use as a recording studio.

larity of this venture resulted in the company being invited to perform at the open air theatre at the exclusive Ranelagh Club at Barn Elms.

After a summer break, Ridgeway had his first success when he persuaded Thomas Hardy to allow the production at Barnes of the novelist's own dramatisation of *Tess of the D'Urbevilles*. The young Gwen Ffrangcon-Davies scored an immediate success in the title role and after an extended run at Barnes the production transferred to the Garrick Theatre in the west end.

Ridgeway engaged the 17-year-old Hugh 'Binkie' Beaumont as business manager. Beaumont, an enterprising and ambitious man, went on to become a founder and managing director of H.M. Tennent Ltd, presenting many of the most prestigious productions in London from 1936 until his death in 1973.

Ridgeway had also engaged the maverick Russian emigré director, Theodore Komisarjevsky. He directed and designed four major Chekhov plays (*Ivanov*,

Uncle Vanya, *The Three Sisters* and *The Cherry Orchard*), in addition to Andreyev's *Katerina* and Gogol's *The Government Inspector*, some of which transferred to London. Until then, Chekhov's plays had not caught the imagination of the British theatre-going public, but Komisarjevsky's productions at Barnes, with his encouragement of supreme ensemble playing, simple sets and innovative lighting, cast a new light on Chekhov's work and he soon became perhaps the most popular foreign playwright in this country.

Komisarjevsky engaged impressive casts for these plays, the likes of Jeanne de Casalis, Martita Hunt, Ernest Milton and the emerging talents of 22-year-old John Gielgud, the 19-year-old Robert Newton and Jean Forbes-Robertson. Charles Laughton made his professional debut in *The Government Inspector* with Claude Rains, yet to be a film star, in the lead role. In September 1926 in an attempt to repeat the success of *Tess*, Ridgeway present Hardy's *The Mayor of Casterbridge*. Although the director, John

162 . *Gwen Ffrangcon-Davies depicted on a postcard advertising her appearance in 'Tess of the D'Urbevilles'. Opening night was 7 September, 1925.*

163. *Programme for 'The Yeomen of the Guard' at the Barnes Theatre, by the Barnes Operatic & Dramatic Society, one of the most successful local amateur groups. Now known as the Barnes and Richmond Operatic Society, it has put on a production each year since 1909.*

Drinkwater, was an established dramatist, the seventeen scenes, in seven different settings, resembled a strip cartoon. Waits for scene changes were overlong and in spite of the hard work of a talented cast the production proved a failure. By the end of October 1926, Ridgeway had ambitions in the west end – the struggle to survive financially at Barnes had probably proved too much for him and early in November he sold the lease.

The Barnes Theatre would be immensely popular with today's residents, but in the 1920s it was probably considered a bit too "arty" for local tastes and the audiences almost totally consisted of Londoners who travelled out to Barnes. Before the theatre came, there were practically no restaurants in Barnes, but once it was established several opened, serving pre-theatre dinners and after-theatre suppers. When the theatre closed, so did they.

Byfeld Hall reverted to cinema use, first as Barnes Cinema, then the Ranelagh (1932-41). In 1951, as the Plaza, it was closed by fire, but reopened as the Vandyke in 1952, specialising in continental films. This venture, however, was short-lived.

The hall became a studio for television commercials, particularly those for OMO detergent. In 1966 it was converted to the Olympic Sound Studios, where the accommodation is large enough to house a seventy-piece orchestra. It has been used by many top recording artists, and for film sound tracks and voice overs. In 1988 it was bought by Richard Branson's Virgin Group, which completely gutted the interior, at the same time refurbishing the exterior to a high standard. The following year EMI took over that part of Virgin's operations and remain in control.

There is today not a single professional theatre or a cinema in Barnes, Mortlake or East Sheen.

Some Famous Names

MUSICIANS

The two musicians most closely associated with Barnes are the composers Gustav Holst (1874-1934) and Herbert Howells (1892-1983). Holst lived at no. 10 The Terrace from 1909 to 1912. The Howells' family came to Barnes in the 1920s, living first at no. 102 Station Road (now demolished), and then at 3 Beverley Close, backing on to Barnes Green, which was the family home for more than forty years. Howells was President of the Barnes Music Club from its foundation until his death. Both men were Directors of Music at St Paul's Girls' School, Hammersmith, Holst occupying the post from 1907 until his death and Howells from 1936 to 1962. Holst's period in Barnes would have seen the composition of a number of works, including the orchestral suite *Beni Mora* (1910). His aunt, Mrs Newman, ran a renowned girls' school, St Mary's College, on Barnes Terrace from 1898 to 1923, where Holst assisted with the music tuition.

WRITERS, POETS AND DRAMATISTS

The poet and dramatist, Abraham Cowley (1618-1667), who retired to Barn Elms in 1662, is perhaps the earliest important literary figure with local connections. In the middle of the eighteenth century Henry Fielding (1707-1754) was for a brief period tenant of Milbourne House, facing Barnes pond, and it was probably here in 1750 that his novel *Amelia*

164. Gustav Holst.

165. Herbert Howells with Imogen Holst and the Mayor at the unveiling of the plaque to Gustav Holst on the Terrace in 1963.

166. Henry Fielding (1707-54).

was written. Later, between 1783 and 1786, the Irish dramatist John O'Keeffe (1747-1833), lived at no. 30 The Terrace. Best known for the genial comedy *Wild Oats* (1791), O'Keeffe seems to have produced little of merit during his Barnes period if such offerings as *The Young Quaker* and *A Beggar on Horseback* are anything to go by. Another writer associated with Barnes during the late Georgian period is Matthew ('Monk') Lewis (1775-1818), author of the celebrated Gothic novel, *The Monk* (1796), who lived at Hermitage Cottage from 1801 until his death. During these years Lewis was to turn his hand to writing sensational melodramas for the stage, and one of the best known of these, *Timur the Tartar* (1810), was almost

167. Matthew Lewis (1775-1818). Portrait by H.W. Pickersgill.

certainly written at Barnes.

The essayist and agriculturalist, William Cobbett (1762-1835), was at Barn Elms Farm between 1828 and 1830. These dates suggest that *Advice to Young Men* (1829) was written there, as well as his most famous work, *Rural Rides* (1830).

Victorian poetry is represented by W.E. Henley (1849-1903), who was a semi-recluse at no. 9, The Terrace between 1894 and 1896, following the death of his only child. Henley was a courageous and independent critic, the champion of such figures as Whistler and Yeats, and his time at Barnes coincides with his editorship of *The New Review* and the serialisation of H.G. Wells' *The Time Machine*. Tubercular arthritis in childhood had left Henley with an amputated foot; this, combined with his powerful and flamboyant personality, later led Robert Louis Stevenson to claim that Henley had been the inspiration behind the creation of Long John Silver in *Treasure Island*.

Barnes can also claim a well-known Victorian hymn writer and hymnologist, Canon John Ellerton (1826-1893), Rector of Barnes from 1876 to 1884. Ellerton wrote some eighty hymns, including the ever-popular *The Day Thou Gavest*, although none was written during his time at Barnes. The sermons that Ellerton preached in Barnes were published in 1882.

Twentieth-century writers in residence locally have included Major P.C. Wren (1885-1941), author of *Beau Geste* (1924), who lived at no. 33 Church Road, Barnes between 1901 and 1904; and Dodie Smith, creator of *A Hundred and One Dalmations*, who, while attending St Paul's Girls' School in the 1920s, lived in Riverview Gardens.

Eric Newby, the well-known travel writer, was born in 1919 in nearby Castelnau Mansions and in one of his books records his boyhood walks across the market gardens behind Lonsdale Road. Had Newby been born a few years earlier he might well have toddled past the children's author, Kathleen Hale, creator of *Orlando the Marmalade Cat*. Before she began her writing career, Kathleen Hale worked as a Land Girl on that same market garden land in the First World War. A slip of a girl who knew nothing of farming, she was expected to load and drive an articulated horse-drawn waggon to Covent Garden each day. Her hazardous journeys with Prince, a colossal cart-horse, the inspiration for Vulcan in the Orlando books, are amusingly described in her autobiography, A *Slender Reputation* (1994).

Arthur Marshall, the writer and humorist was born in Castelnau in 1910 and attended Miss Wright's School at the corner of Rocks Lane and Ranelagh Avenue. But the writer most closely associated with Barnes must surely be Barbara Pym (1913-80). Between 1949 and 1961 she lived at 47 Nassau Road. For her, Barnes was the archetypal 'respectable' south-of-the-river suburb, always slightly inaccessible by public transport, playfully recorded in the novels *Less than Angels* (1955) and *No Return of Love* (1961).

ACTORS

The eighteenth-century actor-comedian John Moody (1727-1812), lived at no. 11 The Terrace, *c*.1780 until his death, and is buried at St Mary's church with his two wives. Most of his acting career was spent at Drury Lane Theatre, where his most famous part was Teague in *The Committee*. Edward Terry (1844-1912), actor, comedian and manager of Terry's Theatre in the Strand, lived at Priory Lodge, a large house facing St Mary's, Barnes from 1890 until his death. He donated a bell to the church in 1897 in memory of his wife. And yet another actor-manager, Sir John Martin-Harvey (1863-1944), lived at Parkholme, East Sheen between 1923 and 1938 and then at Primrose Cottage, Fife Road, East Sheen. He is best known for his portrayal of Sidney Carton in *The Only Way* (1891).

ARTISTS

The area has inspired several artists, including Turner. Thomas Rowlandson executed a wonderfully vivid watercolour of the Barnes riverside in 1800, and in the late nineteenth century J. Atkinson Grimshaw produced paintings of The Terrace which are full of his characteristic atmospheric effects. There have also been resident artists. The watercolourist and landscape gardener, William Gilpin (1762-1843), married in Mortlake in 1806 and lived at Painsfield, East

Sheen from 1830 until his death. The leading portrait painter of, among others, university dons, Henry William Pickersgill (1782-1875), lived at Nassau House, Barnes Green, between 1854 and 1857 and is buried in the Old Barnes Cemetery on the Common.

The Williams family of painters was closely associated with Barnes for many years. Edward Williams (1782-1855) lived at no. 32 Castelnau Villas (92 Castelnau), from 1845 until his death. His five sons were all landscape painters. George and Alfred kept the surname Williams, but the others changed theirs to avoid confusion and were known as Henry Boddington, Sidney Percy and Arthur Gilbert. These three became known as the Barnes School of Painting. George (1814-1901) lived at no. 4 Castelnau Cottages (177 Castelnau) and is buried with his father in the Old Barnes Cemetery. George's son Walter (1853-1906), who lived at no. 8 Lonsdale Terrace (20 Lonsdale Road), was also an artist, along with his sister Caroline (1836-1921).

The Cookes, father and son, who lived at Elm Bank, Barnes Terrace, were artists of some repute. George (1781-1834) was an important engraver, best known for his reproductions of Turner. His son, Edward William (1811-1880), found fame as a marine painter and also produced fine paintings of the local riverside.

The last tenant of Elm Bank before it was demolished was Christopher Dresser (1834-1904), designer of glass, pottery, textiles, wallpaper and furniture in the *Art Nouveau* style, much of it for Liberty's; his work is currently gaining increasing recognition. Other past residents who worked in the field of applied arts were George Dance the younger (1741-1825), architect, who lived at Frog Hall, Barnes in the late eighteenth century (the site on the corner of Church and Grange Roads), and the pioneer photographer Julia Margaret Cameron (1815-1879), who lived at Percy Lodge, East Sheen, 1850-54.

The German artist Kurt Schwitters (1887-1948), the creator of Merz (a form of sculptural collage) lived in Barnes 1941-45. A refugee from Germany, Schwitters was interned on his arrival in England, and after his release he lived at no. 30 Westmoreland Road, before leaving for the Lake District.

There are only two official Blue Plaques to past residents in the area, both in Barnes. One is for Schwitters at Westmoreland Road, the other at Milbourne House for Henry Fielding. There is an unofficial plaque at no. 10 The Terrace for Gustav Holst.

The nearness to the TV Studios at White City and ease of travel to the South Bank and the West End has attracted a number of well-known performers, writers and TV personalities to the area in recent years. Several are by now long-established residents who contribute much to the community by giving generously of their time to concerts and local charitable efforts.

168. John Moody (1727-1812) in his most famous role as Teague in 'The Committee' at Drury Lane in 1776.

169. Edward O'Connor Terry (1844-1912), actor manager, by 'Spy' in Vanity Fair.

Open Spaces

From medieval times commons and wastes were an integral part of village economy, at least for those who had rights to graze their animals on them. They were owned by the lord of the manor, but subject to those rights. Many law cases ensued when manorial lords tried to enclose a common or waste in order to acquire more farmland or, more usually, to develop for building. The complaints most frequently appearing in the local manor court rolls were concerned with illegal enclosure.

In Barnes and Mortlake the commons have been nibbled away by enclosure and the construction of roads and railways, but a great deal has survived. Those who live in the area are fortunate in having so many acres of open ground on their doorsteps.

BARNES GREEN AND COMMON

Barnes Green and Barnes Common together cover an area of approximately 120 acres. The Green extends from Church Road to Beverley Brook, with the pond as its main feature: the central island in the pond was there by 1837 but does not appear in John Taylor's map of 1783. Well into the nineteenth century it was just the village pond, where cows stopped for a drink and horses and carts were driven in for a quick clean-up after a muddy trip along the unmade roads. Today it is a place to sit and watch the world go by and feed the ducks. For the past twenty-five years Barnes Fair has been held on the Green on the second Saturday in July. The fair, staged by the Barnes Community Association, brings sleepless nights to the organisers, thousands of visitors to Barnes and welcome funds to local charities and organisations.

Once across the Beverley Brook the landscape changes to a mixture of grassland, scrub and woodland, which continues as far as the Putney border. The soil on the former meadowlands alongside the Brook is muddy alluvium, and in the eighteenth century turf and spit loam from this were sold in large quantities by parish officials whenever funds were short. But over much of the Common the soil is thin and sandy with outcrops of pebbles – these are the areas of acid grassland, rare around London, which for years made the Common a site of special scientific interest. Efforts are at present being made to restore the acid grass areas which have become overgrown with gorse and saplings. For over three hundred years the Burnet Rose has grown on the Common, the only naturally occurring colony in the London area. A few years ago hardly any remained but the combined efforts of council officials and the Friends

170. Barnes Common, from a postcard dated 1905.

171. *Children paddling in Barnes Pond shortly before the First World War. The Sun Inn is directly opposite.*

172. *Beverley Brook on Barnes Common, as it is today.*

173. *The windmill at Mill Hill, Barnes Common, overturned by a hurricane in October 1780. The mill was rebuilt and stood until 1836. From a drawing by E. Edwards, ARA.*

of Barnes Common have seen an amazing improvement in the surviving area. The heather which once grew abundantly has, unfortunately, been reduced to two small patches. In the centre of the Common on the highest ground, is the site of the former village mill where corn was once ground.

The Common is now an official nature reserve, managed by Richmond upon Thames Council.

WETLANDS AND THE LEG O' MUTTON SANCTUARY

After four years of tunnelling, on 11 February 1993, the London Ring Water Main was successfully joined underneath Barnes Common on the south side of Mill Hill Road. The now redundant reservoirs at Barn Elms became available for a new use. They had long attracted migrant birds over winter, and the decision was made to turn the site into a Wildfowl and Wetlands Trust Centre, the first of its kind in an urban setting, with extensive lagoons, reed beds, grazing marshes and observation hides. Work is progressing steadily and the centre will be named after the man whose brainchild it was, the late Sir Peter Scott. It is hoped that all will be completed by the year 2000.

174. *One of the former reservoirs in Lonsdale Road, now the Leg o' Mutton Nature Reserve.*

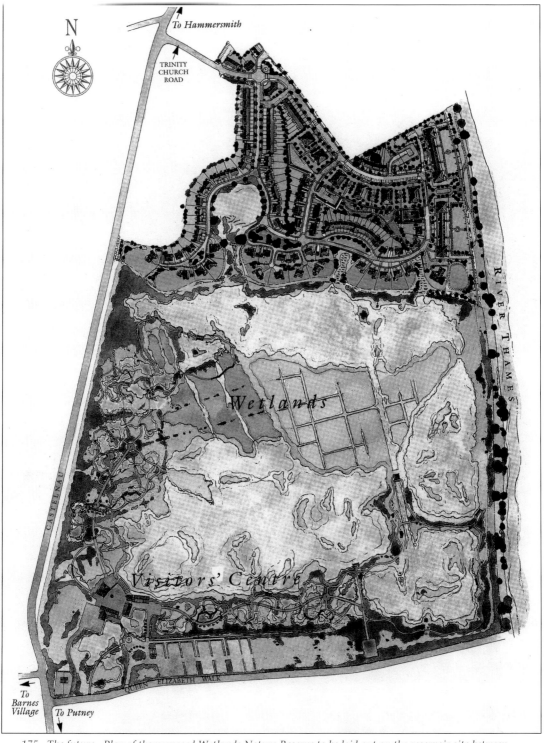

175. The future. Plan of the proposed Wetlands Nature Reserve to be laid out on the reservoir site between Castelnau and the river. To the north is the Barnes Waterside development, presently under construction.

176. Mortlake Green in Edwardian times. The viewpoint is looking north to Ship Lane and the Jolly Gardeners.

The last of the West Middlesex Water Company's reservoirs to the west of Barnes, between the towing-path and Lonsdale Road, has been in use as a wildlife sanctuary for many years, known as the Leg o' Mutton Reservoir. It is an area of great beauty and is open to the public at all times.

EAST SHEEN COMMON

East Sheen Common is one of four commons which existed in Mortlake parish from medieval times. It was often referred to as Little Heath to distinguish it from the Great Heath entirely enclosed in Richmond Park. The southern part of the Common was also lost to the park and what remains outside the walls amounts to 53 acres.

In 1736 Queen Caroline decided to construct a new road from the royal gardens at Kew to Richmond Park. The southern section of this, with the permission of the manor, ran from the north-west corner of the Common to a gate in the Park wall, called Queen's Gate and later, Bog Gate.

The short piece between the Common and Sheen Road was acquired by the Urban District Council in 1925 as an approach road to East Sheen Cemetery, and in 1859 ten acres of Common to the west of the road were enclosed for the cemetery, laid out in 1905.

Also in 1859, the lord of the manor, Earl Spencer, allowed the 9th Surrey Volunteers to use part of the Common for a rifle range, where they were later joined by the Inns of Court Volunteers: an armoury built on adjoining land still stands as a private house. After twenty years of shooting practice, the residents of several houses which had been built nearby began to complain about the noise, but the soldiers were only removed when the residents paid the price for peace – £1,000 to the Volunteers for loss of shooting rights, and £2,500 to Earl Spencer for the land itself.

To manage the Common, the resident owners formed a company called the East Sheen Common Preservation Society Ltd, but in 1896 the newly-formed Urban District Council was approached by certain ratepayers requesting it to take over the management. The Society raised no objection provided it received £600 to pay off its mortgage. Though the management was carried out by the Council (and is still done so by its successors, the Borough Council), the Society retained the freehold until 1909, when it was conveyed to the National Trust.

In recent years a volunteer group, the Friends of East Sheen Common, have joined with council officials in conservation work.

177. *The entrance to Sheen Common, c.1900.*

178. *Paddling pond at the entrance to Palewell Common in the 1930s. It has now been filled in.*

179. Adams or Owens Pond, Richmond Park. The scene is a short distance from Sheen Gate. The alternative names of the pond both stem from residents of Sheen Cottage, seen in this lithograph by the wall of the Park. Lithograph from a drawing by J. Erxleben.

PALEWELL COMMON AND FIELDS

Palewell Common is the smallest of Mortlake's original four commons. There are references in the manorial records to a "place called the Pale" in the sixteenth century, indicating an area enclosed by a fence. Its area was once thirty acres, but of these, twelve were taken into Richmond Park in 1637.

In 1881 the lord of the manor, Earl Spencer, transferred all his interest in the Common to the owners of the adjoining land on the west side, Frederick Wigan of Clare Lawn and Herbert Reeves of Fern Bank (later Enmore), and subsequently the Wigan family acquired the whole interest. Wigan died in 1907 and in 1913 residents presented a memorial to the Urban District Council asking it to apply for a Scheme of Management for the common land under the Metropolitan Commons Act. The Wigan trustees wanted £1,500 compensation for the loss of their common rights, but the Council's limit was £300 and so the matter was dropped. But in 1920 the Council decided to apply for a Scheme and pay the reduced sum of £900 agreed by the Wigan Trustees. The conveyance to the Council was completed in 1921 but still no Scheme was ever made. Instead, and despite a petition from local residents, the Council proceeded to destroy the northern half of the Common by constructing a road across it and stripping and levelling the land for tennis courts. With or without a Scheme these works exceeded the Council's powers, but no action was taken and they were completed. Thirteen years later the error was discovered, and a management scheme was sealed and confirmed by Act of Parliament in 1935.

Lying between Palewell Common and the Beverley Brook, Palewell Fields, some 28 acres, were formerly called Park Mead to the north and Pond Mead to the south. For many years they formed part of the grounds of Clarence House in Priory Lane, Roehampton. They were purchased by the Council in 1920 from the executors of the banker, Hugh Colin Smith, for £12,250.

The Sporting Life

ON THE RIVER

Rowing, both by men and women, is a popular local sport. There are a number of clubs, including The London, Quintin, Thames Tradesmen, Mortlake Anglian, and St Paul's and Emanuel Schools. But Mortlake, of course, is famous as being the finishing post for the annual University Boat Race, which has been rowed from Putney since 1845, with most of the course through the local reach. Commentaries on the race often refer to landmarks on the 'Surrey Station', such as Harrods Depository, Hammersmith and Barnes bridges, and Mortlake Brewery. In earlier days, the market gardeners would park their carts along Barnes Terrace and hire them out as impromptu spectator stands. The more spectacular event is the Head of the River, an international timed race, rowed between Mortlake and Putney on the Saturday before the University Boat Race, in which over 400 eights compete

There are also several small annual regattas in which local clubs take part. The Barnes and Mortlake Regatta, held in June is, oddly enough, rowed between Chiswick and Kew Bridge, not on the local reach at all.

A FOOTBALL GRANDEE

The area has had no professional football club, but amateur clubs have played on Barnes Common for many years and still do. But Barnes does lay claim to being the residence of the man who drafted the rules of Association Football and one of its founding fathers. This was Ebenezer Cobb Morley, who came to Barnes in 1858 at the age of 27. His home was

180. The 1913 University Boat Race passing Mortlake Brewery, with Oxford leading by half a length.

Bowling Averages of C. CLIFFORD, Esq.,
For ten years for the East Sheen (Star) and other Cricket Clubs.

Date.	Wickt.	Runs.	Averages
1890	43	159	3·69
1891	57	207	3·63
1892	71	327	4·6
1893	102	444	4·35
1894	72	252	3·5
1895	47	157	3·34

Date.	Wickt.	Runs.	Averages
1896	44	183	4.15
1897	64	240	3·75
1898	39	106	2·71
1899	47	170	3.61
	586	2245	3·83

181.   *The remarkable under-arm local bowler, Charlie Clifford, whose bowling record is recorded here - he took 586 wickets for 2,245 runs, an average of 3.83.*

no. 26 The Terrace. A solicitor by profession, he was an all-round sportsman and a member of the London Rowing Club; he had a specially reserved room at the White Hart, which was a rendezvous for oarsmen, and he played a leading part in the foundation of the Barnes and Mortlake Regatta of which he was secretary from 1862 to 1880.

It is, however, as a footballer that he is remembered. Morley and his friends formed the Barnes Football Club, which played its matches on a field opposite The Limes in Mortlake High Street. However, in those early days of the sport disputes arose between clubs as to the rules of the game, and it was Morley who proposed that rules be framed for general acceptance. Of prime importance was to settle whether the ball could be handled as in rugby, or dribbled as in soccer. After a meeting in London on 1 December 1864, Morley drafted the first rules for Association Football and became the Association's first secretary and second President. He died in 1924 aged ninety-three and was buried in Old Barnes Cemetery.

TENNIS, BOWLS AND CRICKET

Tennis was extremely popular in the 1930s. There were at least eight tennis clubs in the area of which only three survive – today, most players seem to prefer to hire one of the several public courts on a casual basis; the Rocks Lane Tennis Centre in Barnes, on former public courts, is very popular.

Bowling greens are expensive to maintain, and when charges rose the public green at Rocks Lane fell into disuse. It is now closed. Behind the Sun Inn at Barnes there is a private Crown Bowling green – a rarity in the south of England. A green widely acknowledged as the best in the country disappeared beneath the new Mortlake Brewery buildings in the 1970s. Sheen Common Bowling Club, founded on 8 August, 1914, still plays on Sheen Common.

Local cricket has included an outstanding under-arm bowler called Charlie Clifford. Born in Mortlake in 1840, he was a market gardener between the Lower and Upper Richmond Roads – Clifford Avenue is named after him – and lived in a cottage directly opposite Derby Road. He was photographed in his cricket gear in 1900, when he was aged sixty. The photograph also records his remarkable bowling average – he took 586 wickets at a cost of 2,245 runs, an average of 3.83. Cricket has long been played in

182. Cricket team at the Station Road pitch, with Barnes station in the background, c.1913. It is thought to be a tradesmen's club.

183. Prize giving at the lawn tennis club on ground behind Shrewsbury Avenue, East Sheen, c.1924.

the area, either impromptu games on the Common, or club games on specially laid out pitches. Of the two fine pitches on Barnes Common only one survives, maintained at the expense of the Barnes Community Association.

CYCLING CLUBS

Between the wars Barnes Common was a favourite venue for cycling clubs to meet, but long before this the *Bicycle Magazine* in 1876 listed the North Surrey Bicycle Association, under the heading 'Country Bicycle Clubs', c/o the Edinburgh Castle Hotel at Westfields. By 1891 the club was listed under 'Metropolitan Clubs', an indication perhaps of the spread of London. Then, its headquarters was the Lecture Hall in Cleveland Road, and subsequently it was based at the Coach & Horses and the Red Lion. In 1898 the club was opened to ladies. Activities included an annual Barnes to Brighton race with a cup given by Edward Terry of The Priory, Barnes, who took a keen interest in the sport. The Barnes celebrations for Queen Victoria's Diamond Jubilee in 1897 included an illuminated bicycle procession, held after dark, finishing outside Terry's house opposite St Mary's church. Terry's daughters judged the entries and he presented the prizes.

184. The Ranelagh and Pytchley polo teams by one of the Ranelagh pavilions, 1903.

Before Sheen House was demolished in 1907, it was the home of the Sheen House Cycling Club, formed in 1896. Sheen House, which had a purpose-built cycle track, became a fashionable venue where it was possible to relax in the grounds or take part in various sports, including croquet.

THE RANELAGH CLUB

Even more fashionable was the Ranelagh Club, but so far as is known no resident of Barnes belonged to it. It moved from Ranelagh House in Fulham to Barn Elms manor house in 1884 and here continued much as it did in its former home. Primarily it was a polo club, which therefore made it a rich man's club, but even when other sports were introduced it was kept socially exclusive and none but recognised members of London society was admitted as a member. The Club immediately flourished in Barnes; the Prince and Princess of Wales were among its most regular patrons, and it became the most exclusive of its kind. A long lease was obtained and by 1912 there were 2,000 members.

In 1902 the first Balloon Meeting organised by the Aero Club of Great Britain was held there; the first ever bicycle and motor gymkhanas also took place at Ranelagh. There was an eighteen-hole golf course, archery, tennis and croquet tournaments. By the side of the lake was an open-air theatre, behind which an old domed brick icehouse provided dressing rooms for the performers. Additional accommodation was provided by buildings to the north and south, thus leaving the old mansion externally unaffected. The club house, the old Barn Elms manor house, was furnished with antique furniture, paintings and carpets, all of the highest quality.

Clouds appeared in the 1930s when property developers obtained the freehold of the land from the Church Commissioners and then gained control of the company which managed the Club. In 1935 an agreement was reached with the local authority for flats to be built over most of the grounds, and though much local and national opposition deferred the scheme, the Club closed down in 1939. In the end the outbreak of war postponed development, the house was requisitioned by the military who wrecked the interior and badly damaged the grounds, and in 1946 the LCC and the Surrey County Council negotiated for the estate to be used for school playing fields, with a small area at the Putney end for housing.

Compulsory purchase orders were confirmed in 1949, London taking the eastern half and Surrey the western, including the house, but before demolition could take place, a fire in 1954 reduced the old mansion to a shell. The southern half of the lake was filled in and most of the fine timber disappeared, leaving only a giant plane tree thought to be one of the oldest in England. The grotto and ice house survive. The remaining northern half of the lake has been used for many years by the Barnes and Mortlake Angling Club, who recently obtained permission to extend it. New islands with reeds and other plantings, plus a small bridge, have been added. The lake will now be known as Shadwell's Pond, after a former tenant of Barn Elms, Sir Lancelot Shadwell. The grounds are in regular use for a variety of school sports and a new all-weather running track was laid recently.

Wartime Years

A great deal of war preparation in the area took place in the so-called phoney-war period from 3 September 1939 to 25 August 1940, when nothing much happened and there was time to get ready for the worst, possibly even the arrival of the German Army. The emergency services became a common sight: units of the Auxiliary Fire Service arrived to augment the local fire service and troops were stationed in Richmond Park. On Palewell Common fire hose drill was a daily activity; fire observation posts were established on the roofs of Furness Lodge in Derby Road, East Sheen and Seaforth Lodge in Barnes High Street, both of which provided a commanding view of the entire borough and, on a clear day, of London itself.

Civil Defence training exercises took place on waste land opposite the end of Palewell Park and in derelict houses in Hampton Square (the site of today's Sheen Lane Centre). The Local Defence Volunteers (later the Home Guard) planned, in the event of a German invasion, to create a road block on the Upper Richmond Road at the junction with Roehampton Lane

using some ballast trucks and rails abandoned on Palewell Fields during relevelling work. Air Raid Warden Posts were set up throughout the area, including one at the Green School in Barnes, and wardens patrolled the streets looking for any holes in the blackout. A warden dug-out post on the corner of Scarth Road turned out to be almost useless as it was permanently half filled with water.

Everything changed in August, 1940. One of the first high explosive bombs to land in the Blitz fell in Stanton Road, Barnes on 25 August, killing two people. More bombs fell in September, in Leinster Avenue and Denehurst Gardens, East Sheen; Laurel, Suffolk, Ferry, Nowell and Parke Roads, Barnes; and on the Council House (The Limes) in Mortlake High Street. Two people were killed in Parke Road on the 24th and on the same night there were two more fatalities in Barnes in Willow and Brookwood Avenues.

It seemed to the locals that Omes Factory, which was engaged in secret war work, was a particular target. It was recalled that Hitler's Foreign Minister, Von Ribbentrop, had stayed briefly in Barnes when he was Ambassador to London 1936-38, and rumours circulated about his having told the Luftwaffe exactly

185. The Barnes Home Guard c.1940. The location is uncertain.

186. *Members of the Auxiliary Fire Service parade in the Upper Richmond Road with their requisitioned equipment, c.1940.*

where Omes was situated. Whether or not there was any truth in the rumours, the fact remains that Omes and the surrounding area suffered bomb damage more than once. Bombed-out families found temporary shelter in several local schools and halls, including the Methodist Church Hall in Barnes, or in houses requisitioned by the Council. A member of one Barnes family who was put into temporary shelter in Fern Lodge on the corner of Nassau Road, recalls being there for several years after the war, until the house was due for demolition.

Meanwhile, people 'dug for victory' in their gardens, and allotments and large areas of common were dug up to grow food, as were parts of Barnes Green and Richmond Park. Almost all of the 700-odd acres of Mortlake enclosed in Richmond Park were put under crop cultivation for the first time in over 300 years.

New fish stocks were put into Barnes Pond to encourage fishing and children were allowed to bathe. This was all part of the 'holidays at home' policy. Neighbours were encouraged to form pig clubs, which involved the joint ownership of a pig and the saving

187. *An Anderson air-raid shelter in the garden of a house at East Sheen.*

of every scrap of anything edible to feed it. Once suitably fattened, the pig was killed and the carcass distributed among the shareholders. The problem of where to keep the pig while it was still alive was solved by a triangle of land being set aside for the purpose, sited in front of present day Windermere Court in Lonsdale Road. Today it is filled with rose bushes.

The most serious local incident of the war was on 26 September, 1940. A surface air raid shelter in Trinity Church Road, Barnes received a direct hit and fifteen people were killed. During October bombs fell on Richmond Park Road, injuring 28, and a bomb at Barnes station killed one and injured seven others. The last casualties in the area during 1940 were on 6 November, when nine people were killed in an air raid shelter at Sheen Court.

Although the Blitz was to continue until May 1941, there were no further casualties in either Barnes or Mortlake until 1944, when air raids resumed on an intensive scale in January following which some of the most serious incidents of the whole war happened. On 19 February, the Willoughby's, a pair of large Edwardian houses in Priests Bridge were totally destroyed. Fortunately, nobody was hurt but a large number of Borough records which had been stored there were lost. On the same night eight people were killed in nearby White Hart Lane.

After D-Day, 6 June 1944, conventional bombing ceased but the doodle-bugs began. Altogether nine fell in the area, but fortunately no V2s ever landed. Local people became aware of the build up to D-Day by the amount of equipment coming and going at the Ranelagh Club. Units of the Free French Army were stationed at Barn Elms. Rumour has it that they were responsible for ruining most of the statuary in the gardens by using it for shooting practice, but there were also units of the British army at the house.

When the war ended, as well as local men and women in the armed forces, a number of civilians had been killed and injured in Barnes and Mortlake and many lost their homes. Older residents still have clear memories of those days, but today the only visible reminders of the war are the post-war houses seen amid a row of older properties, and the memorials to those who died.

188. The staff of the Mullins Path, Mortlake, ARP Post, c.1940. The shield suggests they were a champion darts team! The lady on the left is Miss West, still a member of the Barnes and Mortlake History Society.

Modern Times

NEW DEVELOPMENTS

After the intensive development in this and the previous century, there has been little room for any more since the last war, and until recently it has been confined to small sites such as the town houses in Swan Court, close to Barnes pond, which were built on a former contractor's yard. The former polo pony stables in King Edward Mews, Byfeld Gardens, are now a mixture of residential and business units, and the old Omes factory site in Willow Avenue is now part local authority and part private housing, some of it sheltered; to the rear of the Tesco petrol station in Castelnau is a small private housing development. Two other small schemes are in the pipeline, one being the old Postal Sorting Office on Barnes Green, overlooking the pond, and the other the site of a former public house built on Barnes Common, latterly the Café More.

In Mortlake, sites such as the British School in South Worple Way, the Congregational Chapel in Sheen Lane, and the former Avondale Road bus garage have all been used for private housing development. The former Barnes Council depot in Mortlake High Street now contains a pleasant riverside restaurant, a prestigious apartment block overlooking the river and small office buildings. The Electricity Works has been refurbished and converted to small business use, and the land alongside is a pleasant green space overlooking the river.

Mortlake High Street underwent radical changes in the 1960s. The old shops and buildings on the south side, which gave it its character, all vanished under a road-widening scheme which transformed the western half of the street into a four-lane dual carriage highway. Currently, several old buildings on the north side, to the east of the brewery, have either been demolished or are due for demolition or reconstruction. For the first time in many years it is possible to see the river from this end of the High Street, but once again, however, it seems that the opportunity to open up the riverside at Mortlake is to be lost as the open sites are all to be developed.

The most recent development in the area is, however, a major one. A whole new village is taking shape by the riverside in North Barnes near the reservoirs. The end result will be 321 housing units, made up of two mansions, large and small town houses and blocks of mansion flats in the neo-Georgian style, all for private sale. The sole exit and entrance will be through Trinity Church Road, which leads to the Hammersmith Bridge end of Castelnau, and there is much local concern about the inevitable increase in traffic. Possibly this is the last major development Barnes will experience for some time, unless plans are approved to convert the former Harrods Depository and adjacent buildings into private apartments.

A combination of land shortage and financial constraints means that social and low-cost housing and accommodation for the elderly, for which there is some demand, are going to be rare, although three

189. The Council Offices in Sheen Lane, c.1960.

190. The Sheen Lane Centre soon after it was built, 1979.

recent purpose-built developments for the elderly have been built in Barnes. These are Diana House at Walnut Tree Close, Lonsdale Road, and Walsingham House and Viera Gray House, built on part of the Lowther Tennis Club courts.

TRANSPORT PROBLEMS

Traffic is still a serious problem. In 1988 Barnes and Mortlake were threatened by a major new road to take through traffic: this would have had a devastating effect, but that era of grandiose road building is now past and unlikely to return. The introduction of a Red Route to the section of the Upper Richmond Road which runs through East Sheen does not so far seem to have made much difference to the traffic flow, and side roads throughout the area continue to be obstructed by more and more parked cars. So far, controlled parking has been introduced only in Barnes, in the Church Road and High Street area, and there are highly contentious proposals for its extension.

HEATHROW AND TERMINAL FIVE

The number of aircraft flights has continued to increase and although modern jet engines are quieter, aircraft noise continues to vex many residents. With the Terminal Five inquiry still in train it remains to be seen how the inspector's recommendation and the Government's decision will balance the conflicting interests of travellers with those of the long-suffering inhabitants of a large area of south-west London.

A PLEASANT PLACE TO LIVE

In spite of these on-going problems, the area covered by Barnes, Mortlake and East Sheen remains one of the most attractive residential parts of London. The green open spaces which have helped to preserve its semi-rural character are each protected in their different ways, so that the general aspect will probably remain much as it is for the foreseeable future.

An unusually large number of successful societies, clubs and associations, covering the widest possible range of interests, is available to a, generally speaking, highly articulate and informed population. Amenity groups have been founded. These include the Mortlake with East Sheen Society, founded in 1969. This was established initially to campaign for a much needed community centre (Sheen Lane Centre). The Barnes Community Association was founded in 1974, when a Queen Anne house (The Homestead), appeared threatened with destruction. Both have since played a significant part in safeguarding the interests of the community and the local environment.

Some change is of course inevitable, just as it has been in the past, but given the commitment of local people, it seems likely that Barnes, Mortlake and East Sheen will remain pleasant, attractive and stimulating places to live, well into the next century.

Further Reading

Anderson, John: *A History of the Parish of Barnes.* (Privately pub. 1900, reprinted Vade-Mecum Press 1983.)
   A History of the Parish of Mortlake. (Privately pub. 1886, reprinted Vade-Mecum Press 1983.)
   A Short History of the Mortlake Potteries. (Privately pub. 1894.)
Asling, Edward: *Story of St Michael and All Angels'.* (Privately pub. 1928.)
Attwell, M: *Childhood Memories of Barnes Village*, ed. by N. Dakin. (Pub. B&MHS 1996.)
Barnes & Mortlake History Society: *Vanished Houses.* (New edn. pub. B&MHS 1978.)
   Halfpenny Green – postcards from Barnes and Mortlake. (Pub B&MHS 1994.)
   Barnes & Mortlake as it was. (2nd edn. pub. Hendon 1981.)
   Vintage Barnes and Mortlake. (2nd edn. pub. Hendon 1982.)
   Glimpses of Old Barnes and Mortlake. (Pub. Hendon 1984.)
   Barnes and Mortlake Remembered. (Pub. Hendon 1988.)
Batchelor, Meston: *Cradle of Empire* [Temple Grove School]. (Pub. Phillimore 1981.)
Bird, D & J: *Archaeology of Surrey to 1540.* (Pub. Surrey Archaeological Society 1987.)
Brown, M: *The Market Gardens of Barnes and Mortlake.* (Pub. B&MHS 1978.)
Brown, M. & Grimwade, M: *A Guide to St Mary's Barnes.* (Pub St Mary's P.C.C. 1996.)
Butler, M: *The Barnes Poor House.* (Pub. B&MHS 1969.)
Crimp, C. & Grimwade, M: *Milbourne House, Barnes.* (Pub B&MHS 1978.)
Freeman, L: *Going to the Parish – Mortlake and the Parish Church of St Mary the Virgin.* (Pub. B&MHS 1993.)
Gill, R.C: *Street Names of Barnes, Mortlake & East Sheen.* (Pub. B&MHS, 2nd edn. 1977.)
   A Dictionary of Local Celebrities. (Pub. B&MHS 1980.)
Grimwade, M. & Hailstone C.H: *Highways and Byways of Barnes.* (Pub. B&MHS 1992.)
Hailstone, C.H: *Alleyways of Mortlake & East Sheen.* (Pub. B&MHS, 2nd edn. 1991.)
Haynes, A: 'The Mortlake Tapestry Factory, 1619-1703' in *History Today*, vol. xxiv, No. 1, Jan. 1974.
Jealous, E.W: *East Sheen Baptist Church.* (Pub. privately.)
Jeffree, R.J: *The Story of Mortlake Churchyard.* (Pub. B&MHS 1983.)
Marshall, Rose C: *Mortlake in the Seventeenth Century and her Congregational Church.* (Pub. privately 1955.)
   Nineteenth Century Mortlake & East Sheen. (Pub. privately 1961.)
Reynolds, J: *The Williams Family of Painters.* (Pub. by Antique Collectors' Club 1975.)
Thomson, W.G: *Tapestry Weaving in England.* (Pub. London 1914.)
   A History of Tapestry. (3rd edn. pub. London 1973.)
Yeandle, W.H. & Watts, W.W: *Churches of Mortlake & East Sheen.* (Pub. privately 1925.)

Occasional papers based on research by members and published by the Barnes & Mortlake History Society.

Brown, M: *Early Working Class Education in Barnes* (1992)
Brown, M., Gill, R.C., and Shearman, H: *Scientific Triad – Edwin Chadwick, Richard Owen, Benjamin Ward Richardson* (1990).
Butler, M: *Barnes & Mortlake People in the Time of Charles II* (1989).
Gill, R.C: *The Growth of East Sheen in the Victorian Era* (1992).
   Richmond Park in the Seventeenth Century (1990).
Grimwade, M: *Shopping in Barnes between the Two World Wars* (1989).
Grimwade, M & Hailstone, C.H: *Murder and Mystery in Barnes and Mortlake* (1989).
   Lost Properties in Barnes (1996).
Henrik-Jones, D: *John Dee – the Magus of Mortlake* (1995).

Acknowledgements

Members of the Barnes and Mortlake History Society who have contributed to this book, by writing or otherwise, include Alan Bushell, David Catford, Gillian Collins, Graeme Cruickshank, Nicholas Dakin, Brian Edwards, Leslie Freeman, Raymond Gill, Mary Grimwade, the late Charles Hailstone, Dilys Henrik-Jones, Valerie Knight, David Redstone and Mike Smith. We would also like to acknowledge the assistance given by Nicholas Fuentes, Pamela Greenwood and the London Museum Archaeological Section. The editor wishes to thank especially Monty Brown and Pamela Freeman for their patience and forebearance during the writing and preparation stages.

The Barnes and Mortlake History Society

The Barnes and Mortlake History Society was founded in 1955. Its purpose is to promote interest in the local history of Barnes, Mortlake and East Sheen and encourage its study. Since its foundation the Society has published a number of books and occasional papers based on original research by its members. Its programme includes lecture meetings and outings. A quarterly newsletter announces all functions and visits and contains articles of local historical interest. Information about the Society can be obtained from local libraries.

The Illustrations

The following have kindly given their permission to reproduce illustrations:
The London Borough of Richmond upon Thames: *13, 14, 20, 27, 57, 84, 85, 100, 136*
Mortlake Parish Print Collection, by permission of the Rector and the Church Wardens: *47, 114, 116, 118, 119, 133*
Cyril Mullinger: *111, 135, 189*
Roy Grayson Ashby: *180*
James Harrold: *185*
Berkeley Homes (Thames Valley) Ltd: *175*
The family of the late Miss Joan Harris: *165*
The family of the late Mrs Sylvia Lane: *140*
The Publisher supplied *36 and 164*

All other illustrations are from the photographic archive of the Barnes and Mortlake History Society, or members' private collections.

INDEX
Illustrations are denoted
by asterisks